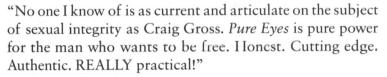

"No one I know of is as current and articulate on the subject of sexual integrity as Craig Gross. *Pure Eyes* is pure power for the man who wants to be free. Honest. Cutting edge. Authentic. REALLY practical!"

—**Kenny Luck**, men's pastor, Saddleback
Church; author of the God's Man book series;
founder of Every Man Ministries

"As Christians, we've barely scratched the surface on a topic that is wrecking so many lives right now. I am encouraged and challenged to see Craig and Steven write such a vital, honest book like *Pure Eyes*. May they continue to speak truth into the darkness that is lust."

—**Jonathan Acuff**, blogger; author of *Stuff Christians Like*

"When it comes to porn addiction, Craig Gross and Steven Luff know what they're talking about. They respect the power of this tyrannical beast and—better yet—they understand how to defeat it. You'll find no naive Sunday school bromides here. *Pure Eyes* contains practical advice for the Christian guy who is serious about reclaiming his sexual integrity."

—**Nate Larkin**, founder of the Samson Society;
author of *Samson and the Pirate Monks:
Calling Men to Authentic Friendship*

"Sex is a gift from God. When this gift is misused, it's either enslaving or heartbreaking—often it's both. As a pastor I've seen many people struggle with the destructive results of an addiction to pornography. Craig Gross and Steven Luff have written a book, *Pure Eyes*, that provides hope, acceptance, clarity, strength, and freedom on the road to wholeness. Every Christian leader—wait, every Christian—wait, every person—needs to read this extremely honest and valuable resource."

—**Pastor Philip Wagner**, Oasis Church, Los Angeles, CA

"In my line of work (hip-hop), the overly sexualized culture lends itself to anything but purity; it's a world that prides itself on misogyny and sexual exploitation. I've been honored to stand beside XXXchurch.com and see the practical and real answers that they provide. It's my pleasure to introduce and endorse what they are doing with this book. I can't tell you how many emails and letters I've been able to forward to them knowing that those struggling with this can find real help for this issue. I know that this book will be able to provide the same kind of practical help that they stand for."

—**Jonah Sorrentino (KJ-52)**, hip-hop artist

PURE EYES

XXXchurch.com resource

PURE EYES

a man's guide to sexual integrity

CRAIG GROSS
& STEVEN LUFF

BakerBooks

a division of Baker Publishing Group
Grand Rapids, Michigan

Published by Baker Books
a division of Baker Publishing Group
P.O. Box 6287, Grand Rapids, MI 49516-6287
www.bakerbooks.com

Printed in the United States of America

Library of Congress Cataloging-in-Publication Data
Gross, Craig, 1975–
    Pure eyes : a man's guide to sexual integrity / Craig Gross & Steven Luff.
        p.   cm. — (XXXchurch resource)
    Includes bibliographical references (p.   ).
    ISBN 978-0-8010-7206-2 (pbk.)
    1. Pornography—Religious aspects—Christianity. 2. Christian men—Religious life. 3. Chastity. I. Luff, Steven. II. Title.
    BV4597.6.G77 2010
    241'.667081—dc22   2010016156

Scripture is taken from the HOLY BIBLE, NEW INTERNATIONAL VERSION®. NIV®. Copyright © 1973, 1978, 1984 by International Bible Society. Used by permission of Zondervan. All rights reserved.

Craig Gross is represented by Wheelhouse Literary Group, 1007 Loxley Drive, Nashville, TN 37211.

To protect the privacy of those whose stories are shared by the authors, some names and details have been changed.

15   16   7 6 5

Contents

Indeed, if we consider the unblushing promises of reward and the staggering nature of the rewards promised in the Gospels, it would seem that Our Lord finds our desires, not too strong, but too weak. We are half-hearted creatures, fooling about with drink and sex and ambition when infinite joy is offered us, like an ignorant child who wants to go on making mud pies in a slum because he cannot imagine what is meant by the offer of a holiday at the sea. We are far too easily pleased.

C. S. Lewis, *The Weight of Glory*

Foreword

The struggle against lust and immorality in our culture really is a war—a war that feels like heat-seeking missiles coming at you every day. You cannot escape the lust bombs passing by, popping up on the web, featured in movies, or glaring at you from billboards and magazines. It's as if someone has alerted the cosmos that you are vulnerable, an easy target, and likely to fall back into the very thing that has brought you the most shame, remorse, dread, guilt, frustration, hopelessness, disconnection, and confusion. The temptations are there—they are not going away—and all of the new starts with more effort are not ever going to be enough to help you survive the war with your integrity intact.

Most likely you have done some very sophisticated research on yourself and have amassed significant data on what will not work in stopping your obsessive mind or compulsive acts. Your research has proven that effort is not the key. Even more effort is not the key. If you have yet to find that key, allow me to tell you what it is: humble willingness. It is not glamorous; it is not something many people are clamoring for, but it really is the key to a brand-new life.

Humble willingness leads you to try something different. It helps you lay down your pride so you can pick up your character. It helps you persevere by reaching out to others when you would rather keep your life in hiding. If you are willing to take the path laid out within these pages, there is great hope.

Your desire to read this book indicates you are willing to learn something new or even try something different. Your heart is headed the right direction—but it can do a 180 on you at any time. If you are humble and willing enough to follow the path laid out in this book, you will live as the man you have always wanted to be.

What we really want is to be men who walk uprightly with integrity and authenticity. We want to be admired for the character we have developed by the choices we have made and the temptations we have rejected. We want to develop lives of integrity where all our parts are integrated together, congruent and consistent and blended into a healthy whole. That is what real men do. That is who real men are.

If I have described your situation, frustration, and desire, this book is going to help you. It is a place of safety and protection, and inside is a path you will never regret walking.

Since coauthoring the book *Every Man's Battle* with Fred Stoeker, I have talked to thousands of men just like you and just like me. We have good intentions and great desire, but these are never enough. We need a path to follow that helps us connect with others, stay connected, and avoid immoral things that cause us to hide and cover up like little schoolboys who don't want to be caught by an authority figure (e.g., a spouse or a girlfriend who plays the role of mother). This book will help you stay the course, and it will develop you into a better man.

I applaud you for reading this far and hope that you will read on. As you do, I hope you will find a new understanding of yourself and what it takes to dump the crummy stuff from your life. I hope you will be able to walk with your head held high or lay your head down on a pillow for restful sleep because there is nothing to hide, feel shame over, or regret.

Craig and Steven are pathfinders, and if you will follow them, you will find the real life of a man. I hope you will jump in with both feet and start walking. And when you are tempted to stop, I pray you will stay the course.

You understand, don't you—this is not about merely quitting sin. It never has been. It is about building a new life; it's about relating and connecting and enjoying intimate moments you have never experienced before. Much of your time might have been spent trying repeatedly to quit, but because you thought it was all about whether you could quit, you could not. There is a big difference between quitting and accepting that you have a problem that is not going to go away by merely quitting. You must build a new life, and the way to get there is by journeying with others over time.

This wonderful book will help you get beyond the quitting and into the living and loving and becoming somebody's hero. It will help you find purpose and meaning for your life and move you so far beyond the rut you have been stuck in that you will never go back. Eventually you will become so busy and fulfilled helping others dig out of their ruts that you will be amazed you were satisfied with anything less.

Okay, that's it from me. It is time for you to step up and step out of a lust-filled rut and into this wonderful life called sexual sobriety.

Stephen Arterburn
coauthor of *Every Man's Battle*

Introduction

Craig Gross

There are a number of good books on the market today that discuss overcoming the lure of pornography, but many of them include addiction to pornography along with other addictions, and a few are too complicated to be easily accessible. That's the reason we wrote this book. This is a pared-down, easy-to-use version of the basic steps any man needs to find wholeness.

Most Christian men have already agreed that using pornography is not only destructive but sinful. They agree porn separates us from God's plan for our lives. We assume you agree and want to end the cycle of self-hatred, shame, and embarrassment that comes with using pornography.

We expect most readers of this book will be professing Christians, but this is certainly not required. *Anyone* can achieve healing by implementing the principles outlined in this book.

However, it is important for non-Christians who are struggling with porn use to realize they may be struggling because they have not explored faith. Skeptics on this point should consider the largest addiction recovery program in the world—Alcoholics Anonymous. Seven of AA's Twelve Steps center on a need to submit to God as part of the healing process. Have a look at the second and eleventh steps:

2. Come to believe that a Power greater than yourself can restore you to sanity.
11. Seek through prayer and meditation to improve your conscious contact with God, praying only for knowledge of His will for you and the power to carry that out.

In addition to assuming the reader understands the pitfalls inherent in pornography use and the fact that he is pursuing or interested in pursuing a Christian God, we recognize and stress the fact that *all of the rhetoric, all of the logic, all of the meetings and support groups and accountability partners in the world won't mean a thing if the person who needs to make a change doesn't accept that he needs to make a change and then take the steps necessary to make that change.*

This book should be viewed as a funnel. At its mouth, we invite and accept *all* men—you—who struggle with addictions to pornography right where you are. Carefully we will lead you down through the cone to the narrow opening at the end of the stem. Here, you will emerge into a new space: knowing how a healthy Christian should think and act in terms of your sexual behavior and what tools you will need to use daily to remain faithful. Men will enter this funnel at different points; regardless, we begin this book at a place where everyone can enter and find healing.

At significant points in this book, we have included questions to help you reflect on your challenge with pornography. These questions represent essential aspects of your healing.

If you truly want to live a life of sexual sobriety, you must understand, deliberate on, and answer these questions affirmatively *before* you move on to the next section. Since overcoming addiction is largely a mental and spiritual exercise, rebuilding how you think, in the right sequence, is key. For example, if a man who is struggling with pornography addiction can truly grasp the concept that pornography is, at its core, a *drug*, the subsequent steps toward healing not only will make more sense but will actually become *possible*.

This book should be viewed as a funnel.

You may be reading this book alone or with a small group. If alone, take the time necessary to grapple with the implications of any given question. Once you feel prepared, answer it. If you are reading it in a small group, let the group's collective growth determine when you should proceed to the next chapter. If it takes two or three meetings to get through a chapter, so be it. Patience pays off.

Chapters 3 and 4 present important information regarding the scientific and spiritual nature of pornography addiction. Chapters 5 and 6 give you concrete tools to overcome an addiction to pornography. *Although it can be tempting to hurry directly to what looks like the immediate remedy for your challenges, please be sure to read this book in order from cover to cover.* To run straight to our sobriety plan without reading the lead-up material would be like running straight to a large construction crane without first learning how to use it—you could end up doing more harm than good.

The final two chapters involve your faith life and a message regarding one of the most important aspects of your recovery: forgiveness. Not only must we learn to forgive others, we must learn to forgive ourselves. Often we find ourselves in destructive patterns because we forget that we are imperfect beings, *incapable* of obeying every law God has laid out for us, in need of a Savior. Even as you begin to recover—*especially* as you begin your recovery—you may find yourself backtracking. *This is all part of the process.* Forgive yourself so that you may grow in self-knowledge and faith!

The apostle Paul wrote in 1 Corinthians 10:13, "No temptation has seized you except what is common to man. And God is faithful; he will not let you be tempted beyond what you can bear. But when you are tempted, he will also provide *a way out* so that you can stand up under it" (emphasis added). This book is your "way out." Stop looking. Stop equivocating. Believe that the principles in this book will work—and use them!

Finally, while there may be some very deep-seated psychological and spiritual issues involved in an addiction to pornography, this book is neither intended nor equipped to discuss them. As you enter into your healing, you may discover things about yourself and your past that are the issue with the addiction, *not* the pornography. Look for this, contemplate the possibility, but please view this book, not as the only answer, but as the initial tool in removing yourself from pornography's pull. Life is a journey, and exploring that journey will prove infinitely more worthwhile than spending hours, days, weeks, or years looking at pornography.

This book could not have happened without the work of Steven Luff, a great friend who has been walking with men struggling with sexual addictions for several years. We have helped thousands of people online through XXXchurch. com. What has happened over the last two years in Los Angeles has opened our eyes to so much more. After speaking at the Oasis Church in Los Angeles one weekend, we saw a need to do more for the men in the church who wanted to turn away from porn and sexual sin. Steven stepped up and led the group. What started out as one group led to two groups. When searching for resources and material for these groups, Steven and I were not happy with what we found. We decided to start working on our own curriculum. What you are about to read has come from two years of work with the men who have participated in the X3LA Recovery Group and eight years of work with people all over the world at XXXchurch.com.

May the grace of the Lord Jesus Christ, and the love of God, and the fellowship of the Holy Spirit be with you all.

2 Corinthians 13:14

Introduction

Steven Luff

One Sunday in 2002 Pastor Philip Wagner of the Oasis Church in Los Angeles introduced in the first of his three services a man named Steve Scholar. I was there at the time, a brand-new Christian safely nestled somewhere toward the back of the congregation. Steve was good-looking, in his late twenties, and married, essentially like any number of the male congregants present at the time. After his name was given and he was handed the microphone, Steve Scholar explained he was leading a new small group, one dedicated to helping men out of addiction to pornography.

The sanctuary went silent.

My first thought in hearing Steve's news was, *Man, that guy's got guts!* But I was also imagining what a pornography addict's behavior might look like, an ironic thought considering the fact I had probably seen something pornographic only a few days prior and would probably see something pornographic in the coming week. As a writer who spends hours alone on a computer each day, I am well aware that pornography is *way* too available and *way* too prevalent, injecting itself onto my screen even when I don't ask for it.

About three years later, after Jesus had begun to radically change my perspective on life, I became curious about the spread of pornography in our society. Why was this very powerful and painfully destructive "drug" allowed such easy, and silent, access into our lives? Was anyone doing anything about it?

As my wife and I looked into the subject, we discovered almost no one was doing anything—not the government, not communities, not even the church. The only real crusader in this arena was an online ministry called XXXchurch.com whose mission was to reach out with love and compassion to those people inside and outside the porn industry who were trapped in a rotating cycle of darkness and hurt.

Through some financial resources my wife and I had available to us, we began to support XXXchurch.com. Little did I know this initial step would eventually lead me to doing the *exact thing* Steve Scholar did—openly offering help to the men of our church who used pornography compulsively and wanted to stop. It all started when a friend of mine came to me for help.

The only real crusader in this arena was an online ministry called XXXchurch.com.

A year into partnering with XXX church.com, a friend of mine, we'll call him Chris, came to me with a personal problem. Meeting in my office one February afternoon, he told me he was addicted to pornography.

How fascinating is God's work in our lives? A year and three months into my own blackout from anything pornographic, God was rewarding my devotion to him by allowing me the opportunity to help lift someone from pornography addiction. Little did Chris know, but I was just the person to seek out. I could see pornography for what it is (a lie), and also, as a researcher, I had begun the hard work of trying to understand this societal problem.

During the next few months, Chris and I worked together as Christian brothers to make sense out of the addiction. We opened our hearts, ferreted through information, searched Scripture, and gained increasing confidence and trust in each other.

About this same time my wife and I met the founder of XXXchurch.com, Craig Gross. He and one of the ministry's board members joined us for lunch at The Grove, a trendy outdoor mall in Los Angeles. A week prior to this lunch, Craig had invited me to their next Porn and Pancakes event in Huntington Beach. As we finished lunch, I felt the need to admit to Craig that, even though I had accepted his invitation to Porn and Pancakes, inside I was silently balking.

I was dedicated to helping the men and women shackled by the lie of pornography, including my friend Chris, but I had to admit I was reluctant to go into a public place where pornography would be discussed. In short, I didn't want to be found guilty by association. What I had to realize, I told Craig, was that to live in that kind of fear only lends power to the very thing that I knew in my heart and mind was working so diligently to unravel the fabric of our society.

So I went. Not only that, I contacted my friend Chris to see if he would like to join me. He had heard about XXXchurch. com; in fact he was currently using them as an online resource and support group. He would love to go! Two days later we piled into his Honda Civic to tool down the 405 Freeway to Huntington Beach, taking that time to talk at great length about our lives, our challenges, and pornography.

The event itself was life changing, as many men who have attended these events can attest. It wasn't a gathering of hurt and troubled sex addicts crawling to shore for a breath of air before being pulled back under the sea; it was scores of men gathered to discuss a topic that affects *all of us*—the sick and the healthy, the struggling and the abstainers, the old and the increasingly younger. Light banishes dark, and I could see in the three hundred or so men filling that wonderful church basement a sense of compassion, understanding, acceptance, strength, and *hope*.

But that's not the end of my story. As we left the event, Chris and I discussed ways in which he could become more involved in triumphing over his challenge. What if he were to start a small group at our church, one similar to the now-defunct small group Steve Scholar had started six years earlier? Encouraged and excited by this prospect, Chris gathered up his courage, and at church the very next day he approached Jeff Borkoski, who was then the associate pastor at the Oasis, to offer his services.

Later that week I received a phone call from Jeff. Aware now of the fact that I had been helping Chris with his challenge, Jeff wanted to know my feelings about him as a group leader, where he was in his healing process, and whether or not I felt he was healthy enough to lead other men through the maze of pornography addiction. Not only that, Jeff wanted to know about the Porn and Pancakes event. What was it like? Was it as cool as it sounds?

For many years Jeff has been an advocate for healthy sexuality among men, reaching out to sex addicts and male prostitutes in some of Los Angeles's toughest neighborhoods. He had wanted to host a Porn and Pancakes at the Oasis for some time but had not quite gained enough of a consensus within the church to make it happen. After I spoke glowingly about the event, Jeff suggested that I do the following: without saying who had put me up to it, the next time I saw Pastor Philip, casually lobby for a Porn and Pancakes event to be held at our church. I agreed.

Five days after my conversation with Jeff, my family and I attended church. There was nothing unusual about the day. We checked our two eager children into their classrooms and headed for the sanctuary. Normally we sit close to the front, but on this day we were ushered to the second row, right next to the stage, with me sitting on the aisle.

The message that day by Pastor Philip was about "elephants in the room," those destructive things in our lives that are so apparent but no one is willing to discuss, like a loved one's alcoholism or compulsive overeating. Halfway through the message, Philip brought up pornography.

In the eight years I had attended the Oasis, I had heard Pastor Philip address pornography perhaps twice. Naturally my ears perked up as he brought up statistics on the subject, repeatedly referencing XXXchurch.com as his source of information. Now you have to understand that I had never spoken to Philip about my connection to XXXchurch.com, or even the events of the previous weeks; in fact in a church of more than two thousand members, I had only shared one real conversation with him in my life, and it most certainly had nothing to do with pornography. Perhaps the oddest thing about this moment was the additional fact that Jeff hadn't mentioned anything to Philip about our previous week's conversations either.

> *The message that day was about "elephants in the room."*

I relate this story not to revel in my own personal "God moment"—we Christians all have them. They're weird and wonderful but they are also real, and as Christians we need to recognize that God *does* orchestrate not only opportunities for us to grow and heal but also opportunities for us to help others in ways we could never figure out on our own. All I needed to do to affect hundreds of people in our church was get up from my seat once the message was over, take two steps toward Philip as he came off the stage, and do what Jeff had asked me to do just five days earlier.

So I did it. Three months later the Oasis Church, a bastion of faith mere miles from where the majority of our nation's pornography is produced and distributed, hosted its own Porn and Pancakes. While it took a few weeks for tickets to sell and a few hours for the men to actually show up, I can honestly attest to the fact that the event has begun to lift the stigma and silence that perpetuates pornography use in our church. I know this for a fact, because after that event we started a sexual addiction recovery group that has grown to include over seventy men. This group offers two meeting times per week. In addition to that, in the summer of 2009, I taught an extensive six-week class at the Oasis on sexual addiction. Through my experiences with these men, groups, and classes, the principles outlined in this book were formed and tested.

Many men in America today, *especially Christian men*, are deathly afraid of admitting to their challenges with pornography. Not only that, even Christian men who abstain from pornography are often unwilling to offer comfort and guidance to those caught up in it; they're even hesitant to speak out against it. I was one of those reluctant Christian men. God helped me understand the degree to which pornography is bad for the soul, yet as I look back at the stories I recount here, it took me *years* to get to a point where I was willing to do what God was so patiently nudging me to do all along.

> *Here's the bottom line, men:* God always wins.

What God has laid before me is different from what he will lay out before you. For some their act of courage and faithfulness in regard to pornography will simply be admitting to themselves that they have a problem with it and taking the necessary steps to seek healing; for others it will be offering their talents to lead men toward sexual purity and freedom. God will use you, just as he has used Craig Gross, Steve Scholar, my friend Chris, me, and countless other men across this country who have offered an opposing voice to pornography's destructive power. We all have a part to play in this, and it begins with trusting Jesus to come clean on his promise: "My grace is sufficient for you, for my power is made perfect in weakness" (2 Cor. 12:9).

Here's the bottom line, men, and we have to believe this with every cell in our bodies: *God always wins*. He always wins. Period.

If you're struggling with pornography's pull on you, if you're struggling with speaking about pornography with your family or children, if you just wish it would politely go away, there is no substitute for holding on to God's Word when he says in Proverbs 3:5–6, "Trust in the LORD with all your heart . . . and he will make your paths straight." Take him up on this offer and see if he doesn't do for you what he did for my friend Chris.

Chris had many things to lose when he came to me. He could have lost the confidence of a friend; he could have lost his standing in the church; he could have lost the respect people had for him as a husband and father. But none of those things happened and infinitely greater things occurred because he dealt with his addiction. Because of his faith he discovered and is discovering his value in God's kingdom; because of his faith he caused a chain reaction within our church that brought Porn and Pancakes to hundreds of men; because of his faith a small group was formed bringing healing to a handful of challenged men; because of his faith *he became the seed for this book*.

I hope and pray that if you are struggling with pornography, you can muster the strength and courage to read and follow the principles outlined here. I am certain they will bring you the same sense of direction, liberation, and hope they have brought Chris and the other men in our church.

1

The First Step

Acceptance

> More than ever, we have big houses and broken homes, high incomes and low morale, secured rights and diminished civility. We excel at making a living but often fail at making a life. We celebrate our prosperity but yearn for a purpose. We cherish our freedoms but long for connection. In an age of plenty, we feel spiritual hunger.
>
> David G. Myers, *The American Paradox: Spiritual Hunger in an Age of Plenty*

Alex had a problem, but it wasn't clear to him until his girlfriend of two years left him. His pornography use, as much as two hours per day, had begun to interfere with their relationship, destroying their intimacy and clouding their future.

In this day and age, stories like this are nothing new. Many men have lost their girlfriend or spouse to their pornography addiction. They've worn out the goodwill of the very people who vowed never to leave their side. Unfortunately, it often isn't until men lose these loved ones—or opportunities and hopes and dreams—that they realize the extent of their problem and their need for help.

For Alex, the loss of his girlfriend was tragic. "I loved her," he said. "She was beautiful, talented, and loving. She was the one who brought me to Christ. When I lost her, I had to open up my eyes and realize that something had to change, that I was addicted to pornography, and that only God could give me another shot at having a woman like her if I cleaned up my life and sought healing."

Three Important Footholds

Alex's healing process has been similar to that of many other men who have rid their lives of pornography through self-examination and prayer. It always starts with acceptance. First, he had to realize he had a problem, that pornography use did *nothing* to enhance his life and had instead gutted his soul. From there, he had to figure out a personal system that would offer him the footholds to climb out of a very slippery pit.

Most men understand. They get it. Deep in their mind they know what we mean when we describe a "very slippery pit." Despite your good intentions, despite how much you desperately want to get to the top of that pit and into fresh air, the walls of the pit are just too steep and too slick to gain any sort of traction. Sometimes you don't even know which way to climb.

While we aren't going to start your climb out of that pit just yet, we *are* going to start building some very powerful footholds that will help your ascent. If you don't know which way to climb, recognize this: your admission of your problem and your desire to seek help are indications that you are going the right way. Keep believing. Keep looking up.

After Alex realized his problem, he had to start rebuilding his mind and the way he thought about both pornography and himself. Alex had to create three mental footholds to get him on his way:

1. An acceptance of the word *sobriety* in the discussion of abstaining from pornography use.
2. A personal and vocal commitment to sobriety.
3. An understanding of his God-given purpose.

While Alex did not automatically articulate these three footholds, especially in that order, he did trip, stumble, and finally land on them at different moments during his healing. His climb was muddier, dirtier, and bloodier than perhaps it needed to be, but he made it. Our goal here is to make your ascent from the pit of pornography use cleaner, smoother, and hopefully quicker than his.

Sobriety

Pornography is like a drug. Similar to other substances of abuse, it alters our brain function, and in that sense, it *is* a drug. In her 2003 report prepared for the Department of Justice, researcher Judith A. Reisman wrote, "[Pornography] is an endogenously processed poly drug providing intense, although misleading, sensory rewards."[1]

While we may not ingest or inject pornography into our systems to get a high (like we would with, say, cocaine or heroin), pornography use triggers the brain to produce neurochemicals that give us highs similar to other drugs. Pornography, Reisman writes, kick-starts "endogenous LSD, adrenaline/norepinephrine, morphine like neurochemicals for a hormonal flood, a 'rush' allegedly analogous to the rush attained using various street drugs."

This may not come as much of a surprise to many men who use pornography. If there were no rush, no thrill in either seeking it or viewing it, then there would be no purpose in pursuing it. It would lose its meaning and become pointless.

Pornography is a drug, and as a drug it can become addictive. In this sense, pornography should be placed within the same category as other substances of abuse, including methamphetamine, crack, cocaine, or heroin.

Pornography alters our brain function, and in that sense, it is a drug.

Do people who are recovering from addictions to substances like heroin and methamphetamine use the word *sobriety* as part of their healing process? Yes, they do. Should we use that word in our discussion of compulsive pornography use? *Yes, we should.*

At the same time Alex was losing his girlfriend to his compulsive pornography use, he made a startling discovery. He noticed that the behavior he was starting to exhibit before, during, and after his use of pornography—lying, hiding, eluding, and expressions of anger caused by shame and embarrassment—closely mirrored the behavior of his own father. Alex's father was addicted to cocaine. "When my dad came out about his cocaine use, I was able to put together that what my dad went through was the same as what I went through when I would use pornography," said Alex. "My expression of shame was the same as my father's expression of shame. I think that was a good thing for me. I never used the word *sobriety* when discussing my addiction but now I see that it was exactly that: just like my father, I needed to be sober so that I could be free of the same destruction and shame he was experiencing."

If you are struggling with compulsive use of pornography, if you find either that you can't control your behavior with pornography use or that without using pornography you are depressed or agitated (the classic definition of dependence), now is a good time to do what Alex had to do, to accept the word *sobriety* in your discussion of abstaining from using pornography. With the adoption of that word, you are also adopting the other connotations that come along with it: pornography is a destructive drug, and you want to quit using it.

> ### ▶ Do you accept the word sobriety to describe abstaining from pornography? Yes or no?

Commitment to Sobriety

All the dissecting, analyzing, discussing, and reading you may do in trying to overcome your addiction to pornography are pointless unless you are committed to seeking your sobriety.

Like many men addicted to pornography, Alex had to reach rock bottom and lose what he valued most (his girlfriend) before he could find it within himself to become committed to eliminating pornography from his life. While it is *never* necessary to reach rock bottom before altering destructive behavior, Alex had to lose something that was more valuable to him than the addiction. Once he figured that out, he was able to find a reason to remain sober: in his case, another chance at a wonderful, God-seeking woman.

You must decide how much it will take—or cost—to be free from pornography's hold on your life so that you can attain your goal.

Sounds easy, right? Just decide you want to stop using porn, figure out your life's purpose, and start heading toward it. Of course, it's much more difficult than it sounds. But let's take a second to flip this around. Instead of thinking that we need to commit to sobriety by a sheer act of force, like a 150-pound offensive lineman hitting a 350-pound linebacker head-on in the chest, there is a way to think of this commitment in leveraged terms, more like the lineman hitting that linebacker low, in his legs, where the size disadvantage disappears and the linebacker is brought down to the ground.

Most men want to be leaders. They want to be the great deciders, the ones who overcome, the *champions*. An unfortunate offshoot of this very noble instinct is that we don't like being told what to do. *We* make the decisions not someone else. And if we've made a mistake, like letting ourselves become addicted to something unhealthy, we're not going to admit to having screwed up. After all, leaders don't make mistakes, right?

But what kind of leader never listens to opposing views? What kind of leader doesn't seek help or admit fault? Michael Jordan would have been just another basketball player if he hadn't understood the need to build up and rely on his teammates to win championships. Winston Churchill's England could have been overrun by the Germans in 1941 if Churchill hadn't recognized how weak his country was financially and how they needed America and President Roosevelt's help. Roosevelt put it best when he wrote, "It is common sense to take a method and try it. If it fails, admit it frankly and try another. But above all, try *something*."

You must decide how much it will take—or cost—to be free from pornography's hold on your life so that you can attain your goal.

The point in these examples is twofold: first, a commitment to sobriety is a lot more difficult—we would argue *impossible*—without first admitting that you are not only powerless over your addiction but also powerless within the universe (more on this in just a moment); and second, if you really want to be a leader, a decider, a champion, you have the opportunity, right now, to make decisions for yourself instead of letting someone else make them for you.

If you really want to enjoy all the wonderful benefits that come with your faith (including the power of Christ to overcome painful struggles), you need to *choose* to accept the fact that Christ died on the cross to set you free. He died as the once-and-for-all atonement so that the pressure you may feel from having made a bad decision or the pressure you may feel to always make the right decision can be lifted so that you can experience peace, happiness, and joy. Accept this gift. Revel in it. As Jesus said in John 10:10, "The thief comes only to steal and kill and destroy; I have come that [you] may have life, and have it to the full."

Part of having life to the full is the opportunity to make decisions for yourself. God loves you, and, yes, he loves being loved in return, but he wants *real* love, a love that comes willingly, from your heart, uncoerced. That's why he gave you free will, so that you could choose to seek him, love him, and obey him. When we don't choose him, or don't choose to make decisions that honor him, we're choosing death, theft, and destruction.

You have the ability to be a great leader. Maybe you already are. However, leadership starts with a decision to do the right thing. The great decider, the champion in you, will get you there.

As men who wish to be the great leaders, the great deciders, the champions, admitting fault and making the necessary decisions to alter the course of your life is not only admirable, it's what God, your friends, and society as a whole expect of you.

We live in a fallen world. We are imperfect people. The question isn't *if* we will make a wrong decision, it's a matter of *when* we will make a wrong decision. But the tragedy isn't that we've made a wrong decision. The tragedy is in not accepting that we are imperfect, asking God for forgiveness, and then making a new set of decisions that honor God, honor ourselves, and honor the people who depend on us. This is what a commitment to sobriety is about. It's about being the man God has created you to be and leading your life with God-given wisdom and leverage instead of according to your own will and through force.

A good example is Chris, who was mentioned in the introduction. About a year after his first admission of his addiction, he came to Steven again saying he had slipped up and returned to pornography. Very carefully, the two of them dissected the events that led to his "acting out." While there were many confusing and challenging elements in his life that could have caused his behavior, as there are in many of our lives, there were also a handful of quite obvious impediments to achieving sobriety.

Chris had come from Georgia to Hollywood with his wife and daughter to seek a career as a film editor. Soon after coming to Los Angeles, he and his wife had another child. Desperately wanting to support his family while simultaneously achieving his dream, Chris was not only working his "bread-and-butter job" as a night editor for a large cable channel, he was also working during the days to launch his own private editing company. For him, this dangerous imbalance of overwork, isolation as a night editor, and self-loathing that came from perceived failure in a culture that idolizes overnight success created the perfect storm in him, which led to his return to pornography.

We live in a fallen world.

We are imperfect people.

Chris had some tough choices to make. He could have thought to himself that, as a man, the buck stopped with him: *he* made the choice to return to pornography and as a leader, a decider, he should accept his "failure" quietly and stoically. He could have avoided talking about his mistake, even to God, inflicting the effects of his self-hatred on his family, then returning to that same exact place he was before—working two jobs, isolating himself, remaining frustrated at his lack of advancement, looking at pornography to "ease his mind," and then hating himself that much more for repeating the cycle.

In this scenario Chris would set himself up to continue his addiction and worse, ironically, to accomplish the opposite of what he had initially set out to do in "acting like a man." Thinking that he, not God, should control his life and not using his mistake to seek forgiveness and learn, he would be putting himself in a position where he probably would use pornography again. If he did not make decisions in his life, decisions would be made for him, like being fired from his job when he got caught looking at pornography at work, ruining his professional dreams, losing his private editing company, causing suffering to his family who rely on him for material provision, and possibly destroying the support and love of the people closest to him.

But none of this happened. Instead, Chris remained committed to his sobriety. He did what a real leader, decider, and champion does: he accepted and admitted fault to himself and God, sought counsel from his wife and a trusted advisor, and then made a new set of decisions to change the conditions that caused his pornography use in the first place. Chris (not his boss, not his wife, not his family) made the decision to fold his private editing company (for now), to switch from working nights to working days, and to dedicate his free time to being with family and serving at his church. Now who is the wise man here? The one who ruins his family, career, friendships, and dreams out of stubborn indecision or the man who recognizes a failing, admits to it, seeks help, gains healing, and grows?

Perhaps it's no different from asking whether you are committed to making decisions with God's help instead of on your own. Are you? Are you committed to being the leader you always wanted to be? Are you willing to overhaul your life completely, if need be, to find and discover those things that may be the problem causing your pornography use? Are you ready to trust in God?

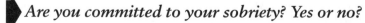 *Are you committed to your sobriety? Yes or no?*

Searching for Purpose

When the X3LA Recovery Group first met, we discussed the word *sobriety*. We discussed our commitment to sobriety before going around the room, allowing each man the chance to accept or reject these concepts. It was surprising to see that the men had a difficult time with these questions—not because they didn't believe in the concepts, but that they were largely new to them and required some time to contemplate and understand. Yet once we got to the third essential question—

▶ *What is your God-given purpose?*

—every man, to the person, eagerly and excitedly communicated what he felt it was.

Ironically we expected this question to be the biggest stumbling block. We figured these men would be very lost, very confused, very unsure of why they were put on this earth. Instead, the fire and excitement that God had put in their hearts for a particular activity, a particular role, a particular vision came forth in glowing and articulate terms. Eddie wanted to succeed as a musician, Ryan wanted to be happily married, both Alex and Aaron wanted to produce films that they had written and directed, Chris wanted to further his financial goals through editing, and David just wanted to honor God.

The reasons they had gotten caught up in pornography use instead of spending their precious time pursuing these very worthwhile activities appeared to be rooted in how they viewed their purpose. Through these discussions, we were able to categorize the three major perspectives men have regarding their purpose and how those perspectives help cause their weakness for pornography use. These three perspectives were having no purpose; knowing one's purpose but going in the wrong direction; and knowing one's purpose, going in the right direction, but for the wrong reason.

No Purpose

It is important to articulate a clear purpose for life. But what do we mean by "purpose"? We mean a destination— somewhere you're headed. Filling your mind with dreams of where you're going is exponentially more productive, and certainly more enjoyable, than fogging your brain with where you've been. The root of this thinking is both practical *and* scriptural.

Practically speaking, when we wake up in the morning, we need to have some idea of why we are getting up. At the most basic level, we get up to work so that we have money to pay the rent, feed ourselves, and clothe our bodies. This may simply be mere survival, but it's a purpose.

And some of you may be thinking, *Maybe I don't even want to survive anymore.* That may be fine for you, but it's not fine for God or the other people who rely on you and love you. Scripturally speaking, God created you for a purpose. There is something out there, a universal need that only you can fill. Paul wrote in Ephesians 2:10, "For we are God's workmanship, created in Christ Jesus to do good works, which God prepared in advance for us to do."

You are God's *workmanship*; you are something God made and is proud of. And he didn't create you to look pretty on a shelf; he created you in Christ Jesus (meaning you are forgiven of sins) *to do good works*! You are not an accident. And just as it is crucial that you understand your powerlessness and need for Christ in this

What is your God-given purpose?

fallen world, you also need to understand that God loves you and that he has a plan for your life. Without you, a healthy and God-seeking you, this world will not be all that it can be.

Because some people feel purposeless, they turn to things that either make them feel good or make them feel pain, even if that pleasure or pain is a means of self-punishment. You're reading this book because you want to stop the pain that compulsive pornography use has caused in your life. Some may feel it would be better to exist no longer than to continue to suffer. But we are here to tell you, right here and now, that not only can that pain be taken from you, but also you have a purpose on this planet that no one else can fill and you can start seeking out and living that purpose immediately.

Just ask Kevin. In his thirties he was so deeply addicted to pornography that after one of his all-day pornography binges, he dug out the gun he kept in his house, put it to his head, and thought, *It would be so easy to end this insanity right now*. Fortunately, Kevin didn't pull that trigger. Fortunately, he sought help and accountability. Fortunately, today Kevin is alive, happily married, and porn-free to serve as a testimony to other desperate men that there is always redemption; there is always hope.

More on figuring out your God-given purpose in a moment; first let's discuss the other two major perspectives men have regarding their purpose.

RIGHT PURPOSE, WRONG DIRECTION

Men, at some point in their lives, feel a tug at their heart. They feel what must be God's call in their life to do something in particular, to achieve some wild dream, to go where no one else has gone before. Throughout their lives they have hung on to this dream, perhaps too steadfastly, or ignored it altogether, and have found themselves either frustrated by their inability to achieve this dream or unfulfilled by where they are in life. As a result of these frustrations, they have turned to substances of abuse, including pornography, to distract or numb themselves. Often this "innocent dabbling" turns into self-hatred, confusion, and addiction.

A good example of this experience is Aaron. When Aaron was a young boy, he would sit with his father and watch up-lifting, emotional, and moving films from great directors. At those times he would think to himself that someday he would like to create the same type of movie, movies that made people cry, laugh, and feel alive and a part of a community. He felt this deeply; he felt it as his calling in life, his purpose.

At twenty-five Aaron moved to Los Angeles to pursue his dream. Hollywood, just like any other competitive industry town, is a challenging place, a place where mere survival meets up with an aggressive workforce to create an environment in which, to succeed, men and women must often choose their career over ethics. To make ends meet within this environment, Aaron became a film editor. Ten years later, Aaron found himself no closer to achieving his original dream than when he first arrived, having sunk further and further into a job he no longer found rewarding.

During these years of confusion, anxiety, and frustration, Aaron turned to pornography as an opiate to numb his feelings of "failure." The more he used pornography, the greater his feeling of failure became, causing him to turn increasingly to pornography, deepening the cycle of use and robbing him of time he could spend pursuing his dream.

We don't know, of course, that Aaron's dream is really his God-given purpose, but it is clear from the Bible that we are all given unique talents and abilities. In Romans 12:6 Paul says, "We have different gifts, according to the grace given us"; and in 1 Corinthians 7:7, "Each man has his own gift from God."

Clearly, Aaron has certain gifts. Not only is he passionate about moviemaking but he is also a good editor and good visual composer. It's quite certain that he wasn't designed to be a veterinarian or welder; that much is clear. So if Aaron is using his God-given gifts, why is he stagnating? If Aaron is doing what he thinks God expects of him, why is he so frustrated and thus turning to the self-destruction of pornography?

There could be two reasons. One, he has been too afraid to step out into a place where he would need to trust that God will provide; and two, *maybe he's going in the wrong direction.*

In virtually all of the passages in the Bible that discuss God's promises of joy, happiness, and fulfillment, it is never mentioned that God gives these things just because we want them. According to Psalm 37:4–5, it is when we *delight in the Lord* that God gives us the desires of our heart. In everything we do, it is our submission to God that determines the results, not our own effort. "To the man who pleases him, God gives wisdom, knowledge and happiness" (Eccles. 2:26). "May the righteous [followers of God] be glad and rejoice before God; may they be happy and joyful" (Ps. 68:3). "May the God of hope fill you with all joy and peace as you trust in him, so that you may overflow with hope by the power of the Holy Spirit" (Rom. 15:13).

In this particular instance, Aaron may know what he wants to be doing, or even what he feels God has put in his heart to do, but he's taking it in the wrong direction. Aaron is still stuck on his original image of putting his talents to use. Through his own limited perspective, he has seen the successes of the directors he idolized and adopted those successes as the very picture of who he is supposed to be. So Aaron's hope is attached to his idols rather than to God, whom he can trust to show him how to use his gifts in a way that is right for him.

Aaron is starting to trust God, and as a result, the sense of failure is lifting.

Recently Aaron started to acknowledge this distinction between his own conception of what he feels to be his God-given purpose and God's conception of that purpose. Taking time away from his struggles, Aaron decided to go on a mission trip to Kenya. On that trip he recorded hours of very moving and meaningful footage of his experiences. As he draws on God, as he asks of God what he wants him to do with his abilities, God is showing him that he can use that footage to accomplish the same thing he experienced in watching those movies with his father, but in the unique, special, one-of-a-kind way that only Aaron can do. Aaron is starting to trust God, and as a result, the sense of failure, which has often caused him to turn to pornography, is lifting.

Right Purpose, Wrong Reason

Do you know that thing you feel you were meant to do, that thing that fires your heart, that dream that just won't go away? You may have been blessed with successes and opportunities in that particular field and this has confirmed your dream. But despite your success, you are drawn to pornography. You have discovered that knowing your God-given purpose and appearing to be going in the right direction with it don't preclude your desire to use porn.

There are very real physiological reasons for this; after all, we are discussing an addiction. But apart from the physiological reasons for compulsive pornography use, there are the psychological reasons. Fears, stresses, worries, angers, and other emotions cause us to turn to pornography, even when we are in the midst of pursuing what we feel God has put in our hearts to pursue.

Throughout Aaron's life, especially as he has grown into adulthood, he has felt pressure from his family. They are all very accomplished with academic degrees, successful marriages, and a bar set very high by career advancement. Compounding this pressure is the fact that Aaron's father always wanted to do something creative but never took the steps necessary to make that dream happen. Now this man, a man Aaron looks up to and loves, is a visual reminder that Aaron must achieve his dream. In fact often Aaron's father admonishes him not to miss out on the opportunities *he* missed out on.

The compounding pressure placed on Aaron by successful siblings and a professionally frustrated father, especially as Aaron has gotten older and the urgency of success has become increasingly apparent, contributes to his low self-image, which leads to his turning to pornography as an escape. Aaron wants to be like his siblings and doesn't want to be like his father, although he appears to be headed down his father's path.

Aaron loses his aim when his purpose becomes outward success. Why is Aaron pursuing his goal? Is it to achieve what he believes is his God-given purpose or is it to prove to his siblings and his father that he can do it? More important, does he want to achieve his goal for himself or for God?

Aaron's story helps us understand the point that, yes, it is essential to pursue what we feel God's purpose for our life is; our entire existence depends on it. But we must always keep in mind that our purpose, above all else, is to seek and honor God. Jesus said in Matthew 6:33, "Seek first his kingdom and his righteousness, and all these things will be given to you as well."

God blesses us with our gifts and talents so that we can honor him with them. When we pursue our purpose with the desire to please others or ourselves, we weaken our faith, weaken our perspective, and weaken our resolve, opening ourselves to the self-destructive thoughts that lead some of us to using pornography.

Let's say Aaron does discover that making this video of his Kenya experiences helps him realize the way God wants him to use his gift. If he pursues it in God's name, he may discover it was merely a stepping-stone for an even bigger dream. Perhaps by letting go of his preconceived notions of his purpose and by adopting the opportunities and direction God lays before him, he will discover that the pursuit of his God-given talents had nothing to do with using his talents at all, but more to do with helping him distinguish between the expectations of his earthly father and those of his heavenly Father. In the end this may prove more liberating, more rewarding, and more joyful than anything he may experience as a filmmaker.

Aaron remembers, at the age of ten, catching his father watching a pornographic video. From that moment on, Aaron had struggled with the notion that a man whom he loves and respects was seen valuing something that proved highly destructive to both him and his father throughout their lives. Now, is Aaron his father? Or is Aaron a new creation in Christ Jesus? The mere fact that Aaron may choose to pursue what God wants from his life instead of what he wants for himself or what his father wants for him may lead to a joy far greater than any professional accomplishment imaginable: he, unlike his father, could be free from the destructive grip of pornography.

God's True Purpose

In every single session the X3LA Recovery Group has had, very little of the conversation has been about pornography itself. The conversations inevitably "digress" into conversations about the members' personal and professional challenges, their fears or anxieties regarding the decisions they need to make, what their purpose on this planet is, their past struggles or even abuses, and their relationship with God.

In these conversations, it becomes quite clear that the issues men have with pornography have very little if anything to do with pornography itself and *everything* to do with a poor view of their lives. They struggle with their self-image, who they are, and what they should be doing as men. And they struggle with what their relationship with God should be.

Those who use pornography compulsively could just as easily be challenged with alcoholism, heroin addiction, compulsive gambling, or compulsive overeating. It's not just about the pornography. During the initial stages of compulsive pornography use, it's about finding a way to mask the pains, hurts, fears, anger, disappointments, and frustrations that they face, or have faced, daily.

Like a drug addict, when we turn to pornography, all we are doing is looking for a short-term fix to make life's challenges and fears go away. As we will discuss in chapter 3, the more we do this, the more the addiction becomes about the addiction. It's at that point that we're no longer masking our hurts and pains but are fueling the rewired circuitry of our brains. At this point, exposure to the locations, events, and processes inherent in acquiring and using pornography becomes the reward, *not* pornography itself. We become "addicted to being addicted," which is why pornography is so dangerous, why we want to get to the heart of our challenge with it as soon as possible and move on to the bright, wonderful future God has for us.

The key is to understand God's purpose for our lives.

The key to getting to the heart of our challenge with pornography is to understand God's purpose for our lives. In understanding our purpose, we can set our eyes on something more significant, more pleasurable, and more rewarding than pornography or anything else this world can offer.

The good news is that even if you don't know your purpose, or even if you *think* you know your purpose, the ultimate purpose for everyone, everywhere, is always the same. In Matthew 22:37–38 Jesus said, "Love the Lord your God with all your heart and with all your soul and with all your mind. This is the first and greatest commandment."

There you have it. Yes, God put desires in our hearts and we should hold on to them, pursue them, and enjoy them—but we should also understand God also gave us a desire to seek him, honor him, and learn from him. To do anything else is to open ourselves up to attack and to remain in bondage to self-destructive elements that include pornography use.

The issue here is faith, not whether we get what we want or what we think we want or even what we think God wants. The issue is God wanting our heart, and while he puts certain desires and dreams in our heart, those dreams (which are limited to our own perspective) are not the ultimate goal. The ultimate goal is to find harmony, peace, and unity with

Christ. To understand this is to be free. To understand this is to grab hold of a dream far bigger than the dream we think we have. After all, honestly ask yourself, would you rather have what you think you want for your life but still be addicted to pornography, or have what God wants for your life and be free of it?

Now you need to articulate your God-given purpose for your life. You need to realize that your understanding of this God-given purpose may change and that's good. It's good because it means you are following God's leading in life, not your own. And if you're unsure as to what your purpose is in life, that's okay. Recognizing that this is where some are, the men in the X3LA Recovery Group came up with this phrase: "Even if your purpose is figuring out your purpose, *that* is your purpose."

With this in mind, fill in the blank below. Use pencil.

I feel that my God-given purpose is to _____

_____

_____.

By setting my eyes on achieving this purpose, I am trusting in God to use my purpose to draw me closer to him, grow me, shape me, lead me, and above all else give me something more valuable and meaningful to live for than any destructive substance of abuse, including pornography.

Alex

After Alex lost his girlfriend, for better or for worse, he wanted more than anything to have another shot at a meaningful relationship. While he wasn't healthy enough at that point to want to be rid of his addiction, he knew it had gotten in the way of a wonderful future with someone real who loved him.

"I knew porn was stealing something from me and at that point it was tied to my relationship," Alex said. "I was robbed of something that could have flourished. This was a big, big prayer of mine that I would get another chance at this. I wasn't praying to be rid of the addiction as much as I was praying to get another chance with a wonderful woman, and I knew that part of getting that chance was cleansing myself of the porn addiction."

It wasn't easy for Alex. As we mentioned earlier, his ascension from the slippery pit of pornography was muddy, dirty, and bloody. There were setbacks and anguish, but Alex believed strongly that he could get away from pornography, eliminating the possibilities for using it (including getting rid of his computer), living with more people, and keeping busy. Eventually he didn't need pornography anymore.

Part of being busy for Alex was getting connected to a church, beginning to pray, reading the Bible, and earnestly seeking God. "I put God first and looked at examining my faith as a training session to get another chance," Alex said.

During one of the God Chicks women's events at the Oasis, one at which Alex was serving, the woman of his dreams—blonde, beautiful, energetic, fashionable, and devout—approached him to ask for his number. Shortly after that they were married. She is, as Alex constantly reminds himself, a prayer answered in his life. And none of the temptations that pornography could present to him would ever be more valuable, more cherished, than this second chance at love.

2

Friends in Need

Confession and Accountability

Often people do not consciously know their own thoughts, experiences, feelings, questions, or concerns until they have had a chance to put them into words for attentive and receptive ears. We can find ourselves saying things to another that express feelings, convictions, or supplications we really didn't know we possessed at the core of our being. Such revelations may invoke an initial spirit of discomfort, but one need only recall that it is an awesome privilege to stand on the threshold of the inner soul and the outer world expressed by another.

Jean Stairs, *Listening for the Soul*

Using the word *sobriety* when discussing an addiction to pornography, becoming committed to sobriety, and taking the time to look at your God-given purpose will all get you on the right track toward a new life without pornography. Ask yourself often, *Why do I turn to pornography instead of pursuing what God has planned for me?*

Now that you have started to rearrange your thinking, the next step is to openly and honestly seek accountability from a trusted friend, parent, sibling, mentor, counselor, pastor, or spouse. *This is your first and perhaps most meaningful step toward overcoming pornography's pull on your life.*

> *Accountability is your first step toward overcoming pornography's pull on your life.*

What does seeking accountability mean? It means that you carefully identify a specific person whom you trust and who is capable of giving wise counsel and you confess to him or her that you struggle with using pornography. When you ask the person to be your accountability partner, it may not be important to give the details of your pornography use, but you must be frank with him about your struggle.

There are four reasons for doing this:

1. The simple process of divulging a secret that has been causing you stress, frustration, and devaluation can immediately, in a matter of seconds, relieve those feelings. As you may know, those same feelings that may have originally driven you to using pornography are often *re-created* as you continue to use, thus forming a vicious cycle of accelerated addiction. It's time to stop that vicious cycle, and seeking accountability can do just that. The author of 1 John 1:5–7 wrote about the importance of shedding "light" on our lives.

   > God is light; in him there is no darkness at all. If we claim to have fellowship with him yet walk in the darkness [use pornography, for example], we lie and do not live by the truth. But if we walk in the light [through seeking accountability], as he is in the light, we have fellowship with one another, and the blood of Jesus, his Son, purifies us from all sin.

2. Telling a trusted individual about your challenge can lead to a discovery that you are not the only one struggling with pornography's draw, and chances are, given the pervasiveness of pornography in our society today, the person you are seeking accountability from may have had to come to terms with pornography in his own life. This realization relieves the great pressure that comes from feeling alone in your struggle. The wise author of Ecclesiastes 4:9–10 instructed: "Two are better than one, because they have a good return for their work: If one falls down, his friend can help him up."

3. Since pornography use, especially internet pornography, is so isolating, making it easy to remain under its influence, it's invaluable to be in the community that accountability provides. Healthy communities have the power to spread value and love, two virtues that help many men escape the emotions that drive them to pornography. In the Bible Paul discussed the power of the "body of Christ" (you, as a believer, are a member of Christ's body, whether you like it or not!). Paul wrote, "There should be no division in the body, but . . . its parts should have *equal concern for each other*. If one part suffers, every part suffers with it; if one part is honored, every part rejoices with it" (1 Cor. 12:25–26, emphasis added).

4. Finally, seeking accountability offers you a wonderful opportunity to start trusting and relying on God. As we mentioned earlier, our purpose is largely to seek him, honor him, and trust him, and this may be your very first opportunity to exercise this principle. As you look for a person to seek accountability from, pray daily that God will show you who that person is. Once you feel God has revealed the person to you, trust that when you step out into the light and divulge your secret, God will be faithful in relieving the pressure your secret has been

inflicting on you. Also believe that he will be faithful in directing you to the right person for the job and that he will set you on a new course toward sobriety. James 4:8 promises, "Come near to God and he will come near to you."

Seeking accountability is not an easy thing to do. But remember, you are not the only person in the world with weaknesses and challenges. We live in a fallen world. That's a fact. Whomever you are seeking accountability from inevitably has his own challenges and frustrations that he is trying to overcome. As an Episcopal priest and recovered alcoholic once said, "Everyone is or *should be* recovering from *something*."

It is possible, of course, that the individual to whom you confess your challenges with pornography will either dismiss you or ridicule you. If that happens, you will have discovered something extremely important and significant about that person—he is not someone you should include in your inner circle of friends or confidants. In fact, in some cases, the relationship you had with the person may have helped cause or perpetuate the circumstances, emotions, or feelings that have often led you to use pornography. Discovering this is good news. This is healing. This is part of your commitment to sobriety.

> *"Everyone is or*
> **should be** *recovering*
> *from* **something.**"

If a person in whom you are confiding is incapable of helping you, for whatever reason, it does not mean that person is bad or wrong or out to get you. It just means that he or she is not at a level of understanding or maturity necessary for this task and that you need to turn to someone else.

It is also possible that you feel you don't have someone whom you trust. Once again, feeling as if you do not have a community to rely on could be a significant contribution to your challenge with pornography use. *What a wonderful chance God has given you to trust that when you step out into the world—into a church environment, perhaps—to seek accountability and community, he will meet your request for an accountability partner!* If that isn't enough motivation, think too that, if you can soon get beyond your own addiction to pornography, you can get yourself into a position where you can make yourself available to someone else who feels the same way you feel: hurt, isolated, and alone. There are immense opportunities for growth here.

Testimonies

To help you gain the confidence and courage you need to seek accountability, we are including here four significant testimonies of men who struggled with pornography use, hid their activities from friends and family, and then either sought accountability through confession or had accountability thrust on them. While each of these stories is different in terms of the individual's age and his circumstances, all four of them now express the same sense of freedom, liberation, and love of God.

We hope that, after reading these stories, you too will seek the same liberation and freedom these men experienced by confessing your challenges with pornography.

Brian's Story: A Church Confession

At the age of thirteen, I was looking for some fireworks that I knew my father kept in a gun case. I knew where the keys were and, as I got into the fireworks, I found a videotape. I was not sure what it was, so I played it in the VCR. The next images I saw would forever stay in my head and completely change my life. This was my first encounter with pornography, and, unfortunately, not my last.

It was here that I learned about masturbation, how to be with a woman, and how they wanted to be treated. This was my sex education and more. This led me to how I would treat my girlfriends in high school: like toys, sexual figures; I didn't care about their emotional or physical condition. To me they were there for sex, and that was all I had in mind. In high school the guys whom I hung out with also looked at pornography and would talk about it like it was the cool thing to do. This only put more fuel on the fire and caused in me more desire to look at pornography. It seemed to me that this was what everyone did; it was normal.

I met my wife at a department store where we both worked. She was raised in a large Christian family, and in that sense, I feel as though I stole her innocence from her by "guilting" her into sleeping with me while we were dating. I had some pornographic movies, and she and I would watch them together from time to time. She really did not think anything about it, as she thought it was just something that men did. When we were first married, the sex was great so I did not feel the need for the porn any longer.

It was after we had our first child that I started to look at large, excessive amounts of pornography. Spending many hours late into the evening, I would search the internet for pornography for several hours at a time. When the free sites did not satisfy me any longer, I started to go to the sites that required payment. It was while doing this that my wife first caught me. Looking at the credit card bill, she was shocked to see a charge from an internet site I had been to. I told her that it was a mistake and that I would take care of it.

This was all that happened at that time. I was so grateful then that my dirty little secret was still kept. Now not only was I looking at pornography at home late at night, I was also looking at it at work. I rearranged my desk so that, if someone came walking in, they would not see it and I could change the screen. At one point during this time, I figure I was looking at porn between twenty to thirty hours out of my forty-hour workweek. Often I had to lie to my wife about having to work overtime because I was so swamped at work. The truth was, I had looked at porn all day and had to stay late to finish my work.

The first big turn in my life was finding a church that I loved. My wife and I started to lead small groups in Bible studies. Initially, I asked for help with my addiction from leaders, but they did not seem to understand the depth of trouble I was in and did nothing.

I had been growing in my faith at great strides until one day I seemed to hit a roadblock that would stall me for several months. I started to ask myself why this was happening and I couldn't find the answer. I was at a standstill with my faith and not moving anywhere. I remember one night coming home from work having the same conversation as I did every night with God; however, this time I was frustrated and very angry with him. "How could you step away from me while things were going so well?" I asked him. I was literally screaming out loud in my car at him for abandoning me when out of nowhere I heard in my head: "You know why! *Porn!*"

Our church was having an event called Porn and Pancakes.

That Sunday it was announced in our church that they were having an event called Porn and Pancakes for our men's ministry. The event was put on by XXXchurch.com. I remember sitting there thinking this would be a great event for the men in my small group. I went to the desk and bought enough tickets for everyone.

The week before Porn and Pancakes, I decided that I needed to tell everyone in our small group about my struggles with pornography. This was not an easy decision, but I knew that somehow I needed to start seeking accountability. I needed to get help. But when I told our group, I said only that I had

had a problem with pornography in the past. I never told them that I was still struggling with using pornography and that it was still tearing me up inside. I had taken a step in the right direction but I wasn't really out in the open.

Porn and Pancakes was held on a Saturday, and I met the guys in our small group at church. During the event, the XXXchurch.com leaders played a video of a man named Bill and his journey down "Porn Boulevard." His addiction took him from "small viewing" all the way to having child porn on his computer. He was caught and is now serving time in a federal prison. This scared the crap out of me. Would this be me? Would pornography take me this far? I did not want it to and without being obvious, I cried at that moment.

After the event I was heading out the door but found myself turning around. It was the Holy Spirit who pushed me back into the church where I met one of the pastors of XXX church. I was shaking so badly and sweating like it was a hundred degrees outside. I was nervous. How could I not be nervous? How were they going to respond to the truth? Was I going to lose my position as a leader in our church? How could people look at me as a leader anymore? And my wife, what was she going to do? I was shaking so badly and I felt as though I was going to throw up at any moment.

I knew then that I was not alone.

I laid everything out for that pastor and told him I wanted to end this now. As I was doing this, my very own pastor came up to thank the XXXchurch pastor with whom I was praying. It was an awkward few minutes, then a group of men from XXXchurch came over and they all laid hands on me and prayed for me, my pastor included. It was amazing. I knew right away that God was with me. More people knew that I had a problem; I knew then that I was not alone and that people were starting to help me with it. After that moment it was like someone had tipped the world upside down. I now had accountability in my life. The pattern that I had built up with viewing porn over the years was going to change.

Just then I knew what I needed to do. I drove home thinking about what had just happened and how free I was feeling. As I walked into our house, I saw my wife and I grabbed her and hugged the life out of her, saying, "I love you so much." Then I told her everything. I told her what I had been doing with pornography, how much I had been using it, that I had been using it at work, and that I had lied to her.

I walked away from her at this point and went to our bedroom. Not saying a word, I got all of the pornographic magazines and movies that I had collected and started a fire in our fireplace. As I knelt down by the fire, I took all the items and threw them into the fire. My wife and I never said a word; I just sat there watching the stuff burn. It was like a huge weight had been lifted off me.

After all of this, my wife and I have been very open with each other and have found out why some things were the way they were. Reflecting back on the ten years we had been married, I could only count a handful of times I had been with my wife sexually the way God had intended. The other times I was living out my fantasies I had seen online or imagining other people instead of her.

After about four months of being clean, I asked my wife, out of curiosity, what changes she had noticed in me so far. Her response was that my temper had diminished, our relationship was growing closer, and that I was happier. The next thing she told me set me way back; this is when I realized the damage porn had caused in our marriage. She told me that she was no longer afraid of me.

My wife? Afraid of me!

She proceeded to tell me that she had felt as though she couldn't do anything without me somehow trying to have sex with her. She would go to bed early and fake that she was sleeping so that I would leave her alone or wait until I was in bed and asleep. I had made our own marriage a real-life nightmare for her.

Since then my life has grown in so many different ways. I now think of ways to spend more time with my kids and wife when I get home from work. My wife and I are more open and have a better relationship. She is no longer afraid of me in respect to sex, and now it is something that we *both* can enjoy as a couple. Being able to talk to her about my problem has opened a whole new avenue of openness and communication in our relationship as well. We are able to talk about anything with each other.

I have been porn-free for almost a year now. This was not easy but I have accountability partners, family, and above all, God. I have once again realigned myself with Christ. He has blessed me with a better understanding of what it is he has planned for me. I have been able to see his truth and grace firsthand, not only from him but also from others around me. This was definitely something missing from my life.

Chad's Story: A Family Affair

I got into pornography in eighth grade when I found a couple of magazines in a recycling area. I looked at them and enjoyed them but didn't really understand their purpose until I was in a health class in school. The instructors were telling the boys that masturbation was normal and not to worry if you do it. I never really thought about masturbation until that time so I went home and basically did it. Well, if it's normal, let me see what it's all about.

That was my entry into pornography and masturbation. Over the years that's all it ever was for me. I liked pornography and looking at naked women. It never got to be an affair or a physical relationship with someone else. It was always just being lost in fantasy and that was kind of where the excitement and ecstasy were for me.

In my early twenties I continued to look at pornographic magazines. I got married when I was twenty-two and didn't stop looking at pornography at that time. I became a very good liar and very good at deceiving people and kept my activities very much hidden in the closet. I had a great facade going of being the good Christian guy, who grew up in a Christian home, who spoke in front of small groups, and who led Sunday school classes—all of this while I was living a secondary life of using pornography.

Toward the end of my twenties, with internet pornography now available, I would look at porn five to six days a week in some form or another for one to two hours at a time. Sure there would be times that I would go a week, or the odd time a month, without looking, but over the course of a couple of years, it would have to be more like almost every day.

I had a great facade going of being the good Christian guy.

There were many, many times when I would act out on the pornography and masturbate, then I would feel shame and I would tell myself, *That's it; you're done.* And then I would "white knuckle it" and go for one or two weeks, maybe one or two months, when I wouldn't look and I wouldn't do it, but I would always come back to it. Always. So there were many times I would try to get over it without any accountability, without any real amputating of my sin, and it was always kind of there, available to me. I would just not acknowledge it for a while. But I wouldn't have any tools to stop from doing it, like accountability.

I'm thirty-six now and six years ago, when I was thirty, everything really came to a head for the final time. It was Christmastime and I had my mom, my dad, my brother, my sister, my brother's two kids, my grandma, my aunt, and then of course my immediate family—twelve or thirteen people—in my thirteen-hundred-square-foot house. There was nowhere really to go, and these people were in my house for three or four days.

On my way home from work one of those days, I was filling up my gas tank at a gas station. I had a couple hours I knew I could kill and right next door to the gas station was a strip club, which maybe I frequented two to three times a year. It wasn't a very common thing for me, as I didn't want to spend the money, but that day I thought it would be a good idea if I went in and sat down and saw some naked women for a bit.

So I'm in there. I had just gotten a camera phone and because I wasn't very savvy, I guess, about what to do at strip clubs, I thought it would be cute if I took a picture of a couple of the girls on my new camera phone. Well, the bouncer saw me doing this and he grabbed my phone.

So here I am: I need to get home for dinner—again, there are thirteen people waiting at the house—and this bouncer at this strip club has my cell phone. So I'm panicking a little bit and trying to figure out how to get my cell phone back. And while I'm doing this, the bouncer has been going through my address book and saw "Home." So he actually calls my house from the strip club and my wife answered the phone and this guy said, "Hey, this is 'Bob' from [a strip club]. I've got your husband here taking dirty pictures of naked women. What do you want me to do with him?"

So my wife thought this was a big joke and this and that, but the guy made her believe him. I didn't know this guy had called my wife and, when I finally got my phone back, I drove home panicking because I'm pretty late, and I call my wife, lying through my teeth, and she's like, "Where are you, what have you been doing?" trying to get me to tell her what had happened. And I wouldn't tell her, and I went down that whole path of proving that I was not lying to her.

And then I got home and, you know, you can't hide it. There's my sin all in front of basically my entire family. Of course everyone knew something was going on. My wife was incredibly upset, and so I had to tell everyone then and there what was going on. My entire life's problem came out at that point.

That was the hardest step: having people know and having my sin, my shame, all brought to light in front of people. That was a hard, hard day.

From that point on, I thought, *It can't get a whole lot worse*. Everybody knew, but what I soon found out was that they accepted me. These people *loved* me. They didn't like what I did, but no one walked out and left my house and never wanted to have anything to do with me again. No one thought, *You're the most disgusting guy I ever met in my life*. They kind of rallied around me and wanted to help me and push me forward and get me to get help.

So it was an incredibly hard day, a shameful day and a lot of sadness, but I wasn't really angry at the bouncer to be quite honest with you. As it turns out, that day was probably the best day of my life, outside of my kids being born and being married to my wife. That was a pinnacle of my life and it will reverberate until the day I die.

That day taught me that I needed people walking alongside me.

Healing hasn't been real easy. There have been hiccups in the road. But that day taught me that I needed help, and help needs to be in the form of people walking alongside me and with me. It needs to be in the form of being honest because, if I'm not honest, I'm going to go right back into using pornography.

Pornography is a sin, nothing else, and once that sin is brought into light, *continually*, its power diminishes and it doesn't have the hold on you that it used to. I don't have to go to it anymore; I don't desire it like I did. Do I think about it? Sure. Does the devil still want to pounce on me there? Absolutely. But I have victory there. I know how to have victory. And I've worked at getting victory and I enjoy talking about it, whereas a short time after I came out, it was incredibly hard for me to say the word *addiction* and to talk about "sexual addiction."

Being on this side of it, five or six years removed from it, I know I was absolutely, completely, addicted to it. Now I consider that part of Chad as dead. I'm a dead man. It's pretty hard to kick a dead man. When people know about who I am and what I really did and that kind of thing, I mean, you can't tear me down much lower.

Before, I didn't want anybody to know about my struggles. Now I tell everybody, for the most part, because it's who I am.

I read a quote that everybody needs to deal with struggles in their lives; you have struggles in your life and if you're not dealing with a struggle, you should be. So a lot of people look at me now as strong. Instead of feeling weak and ashamed, walking with my tail between my legs, I am the one walking tall because I know who I am. And that's been one of my experiences. People are drawn to me. There's power in confessing your sins. It's more than incredible; it's life altering.

Bill's Story: Pastors Struggle Too

My mom and dad divorced when I was a kid. She was a conservative Southern Baptist fundamentalist and my dad was a postmodern existential pantheist, at least he was at the time. Pornography always had a hold on my dad, and I think that was one of the reasons my parents divorced.

One of my earliest memories of being exposed to pornography, publicly even, was when my dad would have friends over when I was nine years old. He had a laser disk player and he had *Playboy* disks that he would show to all of his friends with me in the room. This exposure kind of escalated from there when he wanted to teach me about sex. His way of doing it was giving me a *Playboy* magazine, which was the complete opposite of what my mom would do.

I was always kind of able to have my wits about me. I accepted Christ when I was young. I was about eight years old. This was right before a lot of the exposure. For a long time I was able to know that pornography was wrong. I felt the conviction of the Spirit and so I would just chalk it up as my dad just being my dad, and it didn't really end up having that much of an impact on me.

But then, when I was about fourteen or fifteen, I spent a summer with my dad and I discovered some of his VHS or Beta pornography tapes. Now this was totally different because this wasn't just still photography, this was hardcore porn. I was extremely curious, because though I kind of knew what sex was, I had no idea how it all worked. I even remember praying to God, "Please protect me through this. I'm just curious." But the problem was it was way more intense than anything I had ever seen, and I think this was the first time I had ever conceptualized things like oral sex.

And I think that really struck me emotionally. You know, they talk about the effect that stuff can have on you chemically, that it lasts with you, almost like the first hit of crack or something for people who wrestle with it. That was a moment in time that really stuck with me.

When I was fifteen, I felt like God was really clamping down on me as far as purity goes and I started to feel conviction about certain things in my life, including masturbation and pornography. My future wife and I were high school sweethearts and, after dating for five years, we got married. We were both virgins when we married, and I didn't masturbate during the time right before our marriage. I completely stopped looking at anything sexual. I even stopped watching movies that were above PG-13.

All was good until I was in my late twenties, early thirties. I'm a pastor and one of my co-workers was caught in his addiction to pornography. I was there to help him, but it's like the apostle Paul wrote, "Watch yourself, or you also may be tempted" (Gal. 6:1). In helping him, I felt like a scab got picked back off my life. I had loosened some of my own personal boundaries as far as what I watched and that opened the door for pornography. But now pornography viewing was in a whole new context. I had the internet, and *everything* was available to me now.

At this same time my wife gave birth to our second child. Sexually she was less available, and we were struggling as a couple. If you add all of those factors together, pornography became an option. So I found myself using it again. Two to three times a week I would find myself in places I shouldn't be online. My habit was like Lot from the Old Testament. I would get right up to the border of things, only rarely diving in all the way.

So I would look up things like "sexual positions" under the auspices of "helping our marriage" and I would end up seeing, of course, pictures of couples engaging in sex. I never masturbated to any of it, just viewed it. But the problem was the disconnect between what I *knew* I should do and what I was *not* doing—being obedient to God. Then I would periodically view a "free" video clip of oral sex or something, and that's when I knew something had to change. I was crossing a line into things that were going to be very destructive.

As far as accountability went, I didn't really feel like I had anybody, locally in my churches or anything, with whom I could talk. I had already seen what had happened to my friend when he got caught with pornography. I felt like I just needed to clamp down and get this dealt with, and I felt like the only person I really had to talk to at the time was my wife.

I was afraid at first. There's that weak feeling of brokenness that comes by the Spirit when you come clean and you're confessional. It's a weird feeling. I felt a whole lot of peace and I also felt a whole lot of love because of the way she received me. If I hadn't, if I just kept burying it, I imagine the problem would have gotten a lot worse and probably gotten to the point where, I don't know, she wouldn't have been so kind.

And it was risky because my wife could have wanted to divorce me, but in my wife's case she was like, "We'll work through this. I want to know when you're seeing it. What you're seeing." And the thought that she knew that and would be asking helped me get clear of it. But in time, once some distancing occurred from that, I was able to establish more accountability in my life. Once there was a little bit of distance in time, I started building deeper friendships outside of my local ministry.

My wife said, "We'll work through this."

I don't want to be so brash as to say that I'm completely dead to it. I would say I'm *dying* to it. Always, like an alcoholic, it's going to be around and you have to be conscious of it. I wish that it had never happened the second time, but I think it was important that it did. As a pastor I think the second time around has given me the understanding that I need to become more public. There needs to be a certain amount of transparency on my part to help others. I speak about pornography publicly a lot because these are the things that people in my congregation are dealing with. And if I don't address them and hit these issues full force, a lot of them are going to continue.

I had a guy confess to me a month ago that this has been a problem since he was eight and he was in tears. I said, "Brother, why are you crying?" And he said, "Because I thought you wouldn't be my friend anymore." And I said, "Are you kidding me? I love you with all my heart. I totally don't see you any different than before. You're my brother and nothing changes." He has that belief about himself that he's not lovable because of his porn use and that belief needs to be shattered.

Peter's Story: A Teenager's Odyssey

I've been struggling with pornography since I was ten. It started supersmall, like little inserts in Sunday ads, and very rarely too. Then it grew. Not until I was sixteen did I get involved in the soft-core stuff, the stuff that sticks around for a while. You know what I'm talking about, the stuff that keeps you from hanging out with your friends because "I'm busy right now, maybe later," the kind of stuff that keeps you up late at night and forces you to sleep at school or later in the afternoon the next day (messing up your internal clock to no end), the kind of stuff that makes you so ashamed that every time your parents call your name, you just want to hide for fear they caught you, the kind of stuff that'll draw you in, week after tormenting week.

During those years I wanted to get out of this rut. I'd fight it, get angry at myself every time I'd stumble, and wonder why I was even stumbling at all. I'm fighting it. I'm reading my Bible. I'm praying. But did I honestly jump in all the way? Did I really embrace the change? Did I remove *everything* that could cause me temptation? I didn't. I thought, *I'll just hold on to this until I beat it. Then it won't be a problem anymore. I can look at this and not be tempted*. But after falling so many times, after so many false hopes, I just sort of didn't care anymore. I just sort of hoped it would go away on its own.

But finally I made a choice. One thing I had neglected to do was confess to the people I'd wronged in my sin: my parents. It took some courage, and I've got to admit that I was a bit scared having to bring this up to them again. But after doing just that, I feel this weight is lifted. I feel *better* for having done it. Seriously, if you want to get better, you have to shine the light on your sin. If you don't, it'll just grow and grow; and week after pathetic week you'll fall and fall and fall and fall. It's really not as painful as you think. You just have to be 100 percent honest.

Here's my letter to my parents:

> I have a bit of a confession to make. This is part of a 60-day purity course I'm taking online. So here goes:

I need to apologize to you and dad for abusing what you gave me, for, yes, the second time. I've disobeyed you both and God at the same time. I brought things into your home that I know you aren't happy with. Being a teenage guy is difficult in the world we live in. And more than you'd like to believe, probably nine out of ten guys struggle with this problem. I don't want you to freak out and go crazy. It IS a serious issue, but it has to be handled properly. The last time you disconnected me, I still dealt with it every day. I found other ways to vent the pressure. So, cutting me off the Internet . . . it's not solving the problem. I do realize that the Internet is the easiest, fastest way to get into trouble, and that the simple solution is to just throw it out.

Period.

For good.

I get that.

It's the best way to kill it so I won't deal with this, right?

Wrong. The feelings don't go away just because the Internet is gone. It takes more than that to want to change.

Now on the topic of change:

I have since deleted everything that could cause problems for me. Like absolutely everything. My entire anime collection (50gb or so) is deleted. Granted, there wasn't anything bad in there, but it caused temptations.

My wallpaper collection is gone too. There was some stuff in there, not overtly bad, but again, caused temptations.

I'm seriously considering burning a few of my mangas that have caused temptations for me also. (Day 5 of my Internet purity course said to be radical about removing it *all*. So I'm going to do just that. Also, XXXchurch.com said to have fun with your "removal.")

I've installed a very good Internet filter, which I won't mess with once it's in place.

I'm talking to my Internet purity course mentor every day.

I'm going to talk to [my brother-in-law] every day. He's going to check up on me *every* day and make sure that I'm not messing up and I'm not wasting my day sitting on the computer. He's even told me it's OK to text him right when

I'm hit with any sort of temptation and he'll help me process it. We just discussed doing this today. He's probably the best person for me to talk to until I get my car and can go to church by myself.

I'm determined to actually see this through to the end. I'm so done with this feeling it leaves me with inside.

But basically, this is part of my Day 4 objective in that course. I delayed doing this for a day or two because I figured the outcome would be that my Internet access would be shut off, and I would no longer be able to continue the course or talk to [my brother-in-law] on AIM or (God forbid) play World of Warcraft (which is going to expire on the 15th, don't worry, I won't pick it back up).

It's OK to text him right when I'm hit with any sort of temptation.

I remember what happened last time, what with the high blood pressure and all. This is why I'm being vague. And you have to . . . *have to* . . . understand that this is something I need to deal with. I have to push through this if I want to change the state of my heart and really honestly want to glorify God in each day I live. I have to push through this so that I'll be in control when I move out. Even if it means falling down a few times to get there.

The thing I would absolutely hate is for this to be put off until later when I move out. That's why I'm dealing with this now. Because if I had to start dealing with this problem when I move out . . . it could cause far more drastic issues (problems in an office setting, problems with women, etc.). I'm really on the up and up about this. I want this to be dealt with now, while I'm single and I don't have all that much responsibility. That way, I'll be far better off in the future.

All I ask of you are two things: one, your forgiveness for breaking the rules again. Two, that you subtly help out. (As in, you know, make sure I'm not keeping my door closed. Making sure I'm not spending too much time alone. If that means asking me to go with you on errands, that's fine.) I don't really want you to step in and try to fight this for me.

It's my heart and my body; ergo, you can't fix it. I know you probably feel a little uncomfortable trying to let that sink in, but it's entirely true. You can't fix my problem for me. It's something I have to do. I'm also not trying to ask you to sit back and do nothing, but as I've told [my brother-in-law] and [my sister] and you at one point, it's not the kind of thing a guy talks to his mom about. It's just weird.

So take solace in knowing that I took an active step on this issue. That I'm actually fighting to be an honorable man of God. That I didn't just wait until I was caught to let this into the light. Part of the teaching in Day 3 in my online course is that you have to shine the light on these things, and that in doing so, it makes it easier to deal with.

Today was just a turning point of sorts. A way of showing God that I'm OK with whatever happens. That I'm willing to let the light shine wherever it may. Everything I've asked isn't a demand. It's just a request. I'm working this out and I really don't want any bombs to go off. It's like, yeah, it's not a good situation to be in, but put it in perspective (as in rationally, not emotionally) and remember that I'm responsible for myself before God and that only He can help me through this. No one else is involved in that except my accountability partners. Just pray for me for the next few weeks. It's going to be rough sailing for a bit. But I'm being persistent in this. I'm learning how to "live in the tension."

I'm going to ask [my brother-in-law] to talk to you about this too. Just so you see his side of it also since he also went through this and knows the difficulties on the same level as me. Maybe I'll have [my sister] talk to you too.

One last thing. Don't think too much about this. It's saddening, yes, but also manageable. A lot of guys start in their twenties or so after going through some icky stuff that wakes them up. I'm just different in that I can see what will happen from listening to sermon after sermon, reading testimonial after testimonial, and book after book. I'm not ill prepared. I have myself equipped with everything I need to get over this. And it is possible. After the 60-day course, it should be gone if I stay on track and on the up and up.

I actually feel happy now that I've done this. I feel complete knowing that I've done everything I need to do to start over.

Guys, I'm done with porn. I'm going to take this sin out back and shoot it. I suggest you do the same. No sense in putting off until tomorrow what you can do today, right?

My prayers are with everyone who wants out.

Seeking Accountability

There are millions of men in this world who share this same challenge with pornography. And there are thousands of courageous men who have made the decision to step out into the light to confess and find accountability. You should be one of them. You should be one of the brave ones who have stepped out and, in stepping out, have met God and found all that he has planned for you: community, friendships, hope, and grace.

I'm going to take this sin out back and shoot it.

Even the apostle Paul suffered in this same way. In 2 Corinthians 12:7 he writes of suffering from a "thorn in my flesh, a messenger of Satan, to torment me." He too struggled with something that gave him anguish and frustration in the same way that compulsive pornography use does.

Paul's solution to his challenge was not to run and hide. His solution was to embrace his weakness, even to boast about it, for he knew that in his weakness strength would be found. Paul wrote of his challenge:

> Three times I pleaded with the Lord to take it away from me. But he said to me, "My grace is sufficient for you, for my power is made perfect in weakness." Therefore I will boast all the more gladly about my weaknesses, so that Christ's power may rest on me. That is why, for Christ's sake, I delight

in weaknesses, in insults, in hardships, in persecutions, in difficulties. For when I am weak, then I am strong.

2 Corinthians 12:8–10

Are you ready to admit to someone that you are just like any other human being on the planet? Are you ready to admit to a trusted advisor that you struggle with something that almost any man could be tempted by? Are you ready, just as Paul was, to admit to your weakness, even celebrate it, so that you can invite the Holy Spirit in to do his work? Are you ready to take the most significant action step needed to achieve your sobriety?

✓ *Are you ready to seek accountability/confess? Yes or no?*

✓ *To whom do you feel God is leading you for your confession? Name here: _____*

✓ *Did you follow through and confess? Yes or no?*

--- --- --- --- ---

3

So *That's* What's Going On!

Defining the Addiction

Threatened, any of us may dispense with our Christian convictions and values. Anxiety is no respecter of belief systems.
It is an indiscriminate trigger. Threat is threat. The reptilian
brain is not impressed by the sincerity of what we believe to
be true; it does what it is designed to do: react instinctively.

Peter L. Steinke, *How Your Church Family Works*

Now may be a good time to take a break from the difficult
work required of acceptance and accountability. Accepting
that you have a challenge with something destructive and then
admitting it to someone close is not only difficult, it can also
be exhausting. Often life is challenging enough without the
added complication of completely overhauling your entire
perception of it. Of course, the benefits of realigning your
life with God's vision for it will make your life better in the

long run and more fulfilling. Regardless of these rewards, it doesn't change the fact that it's not easy to do.

So we're going to take a break and start examining the science behind the way your mind and body respond to pornography and what causes you to engage in the self-destructive cycle of using it.

Yes, independent from what you know to be right or wrong regarding the use and abuse of pornography, repeated exposure to it changes your brain so that you have less and less control over your behavior. This doesn't mean you can't make the decisions and take the steps required for healing from the addiction (like acceptance and seeking accountability); it also doesn't mean you can't be freed from it. It *does* mean there are very natural mental and physical responses to sexual images that God designed in us, and once these mental and physical responses to sexual images have been abused, your brain attaches itself to these sexual images in very powerful and destructive ways. That's the reason we use the word *addiction* to describe it.

That's the reason we use the word addiction *to describe it.*

According to the Experts

To understand how the brain and body respond to pornography, and to provide us with some understanding of why we can often lose control of our mind and body when exposed to it, Steven sat down with two experts in the field of addictions and sexuality for a wonderfully eye-opening and educational interview.

Dr. Ralph Koek is a clinical professor in the Department of Psychiatry and Biobehavioral Sciences at the David Geffen School of Medicine at UCLA and is also on the faculty of the UCLA/San Fernando Valley Psychiatry Training Program. Dr.

Koek has garnered considerable clinical experience treating patients with all kinds of addictions. In addition, he has a long-standing clinical, educational, and research interest in brain-behavior relationships in mental illness.

Alexandra Katehakis is a licensed marriage and family therapist, certified sex addiction therapist, certified sex therapist with the Center for Healthy Sex in Beverly Hills, California, and author of *Erotic Intelligence*. She has extensive experience in working with sexual addiction and problems of sexual desire and dysfunction.

This interview, which constitutes the basis for this chapter, was a unique one. Instead of getting a one-sided view of compulsive pornography use from either a psychiatrist's or a therapist's perspective, we participated in a well-balanced discussion that encompassed both research and clinical experience. From this discussion emerged a very comprehensive view of what we can currently understand regarding how pornography works on us, how we can become addicted to it, and what we can do to overcome the addiction.

As of the printing of this book, there has been little if any research done specifically on the neurobiological changes of people with pornography addiction. In fact *The Diagnostic and Statistical Manual of Mental Disorders-IV*, the guide that the psychiatric community uses in diagnosing mental illnesses, has not yet recognized addiction to pornography as a specific mental condition. There are related disorders, such as Paraphilic Disorder, Not Otherwise Specified, but nothing is listed directly relating to pornography.

As Dr. Koek points out in our interview, however, a number of correlating scientific studies on humans with drug addictions are relevant, as are animal studies in which animals have been made to become addicted. We can extrapolate from these studies a very clear picture of the physiological response our brains and bodies have to pornography. In other words, the similarity between behavior seen in chemical addiction (alcohol, heroin, cocaine, and so on) and pornography addiction is so profound that it is likely that similar neurobiological changes occur in the chemical addict's reward system (to be discussed in a moment) and the pornography addict's reward system when either group compulsively abuses its substance of choice.

To help you in reading this chapter, we have summarized its most important points and vocabulary below. If you understand these very basic principles and terms, you will have at your fingertips some of the most important concepts needed to overcome pornography's draw on your life.

✗ Exposure to rewards (like pornography viewing) triggers a portion of the brain called the *ventral tegmental area* to release a surge of the neurochemical *dopamine* into three different areas of the brain: the *nucleus accumbens*, the *prefrontal cortex*, and the *amygdala*.

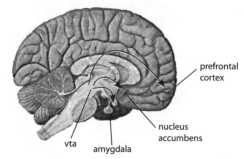

✗ Dopamine release into the *nucleus accumbens* gives us a feeling of ecstasy and exhilaration in the body.

✗ Dopamine release into the *prefrontal cortex*, or the reasoning part of the brain, leads us to strengthen the behavioral circuits needed to pursue and obtain a certain reward. In other words, the more we have exposed our brains to pornography, the more we are going to continue pursuing pornography whether we want to or not.

✗ Dopamine release into the *amygdala* leads us to remember—both consciously and unconsciously—the details of a situation related to a reward. In other words, through continued pornography use, our brains remember the details of the situations associated with acquiring and using pornography. For instance, the sight of a particular newsstand, being alone with a computer, or feelings such as sorrow, frustration, or stress can trigger a deep desire to use pornography independent of *seeing* pornography.

✗ Our brains become increasingly tolerant of dopamine levels so that for an addicted person to achieve the same dopamine high, increasingly "novel" (more hardcore) forms of pornography may become necessary.

✗ Since addictions to pornography are similar in scope to other addictions to substances of abuse, like heroin or methamphetamine, and since some people *do* recover from addiction to those substances, the same proven recovery steps that work vis-à-vis other addictions can help one achieve sobriety and freedom from addiction to pornography.

The Brain's Reward System

The brain's reward system is a handful of different parts that help the brain remember important or pleasurable things for future use or enjoyment. These things could be a type of food, a special event, a certain sensation, a specific person, a particular sexual experience, and so on. While this system has some pretty sophisticated-sounding parts, they are all well worth knowing and remembering.

Dr. Koek offers a quick tour: "What we now understand from careful study with modern neuroimaging methods in human brains as well as from animal studies is that the normal reward system starts with a subcortical connection between a center in the midbrain called the ventral tegmental area (VTA) where dopamine is synthesized and from which it is released with a projection or a transmission or a sending of the dopamine from that area to three major limbic reward system nuclei: the nucleus accumbens, portions of the prefrontal cortex, and the amygdala."

According to Dr. Koek, that's "basically it."

"These structures are deep in the brain," he added, "they're not a part of the cerebral cortex [the thinking part of the brain]; they're subcortical [below the thinking part of the brain], large masses of cells."

The three areas of the brain to which dopamine is released—the nucleus accumbens, portions of the prefrontal cortex, and the amygdala—are affected in different ways by that dopamine release. For example, dopamine release to the nucleus accumbens in the frontal lobe is what causes that experience of pleasure associated with a given reward. Dopamine release to portions of the prefrontal cortex leads to a strengthening of behavioral circuits required to pursue and obtain a reward. Dopamine release in the amygdala, the portion of the brain that integrates sensory information such as sight, hearing, touch, smell, and taste with emotional information, causes us to remember the details of a situation associated with a reward, such as places, people, smells, and such.

"What this [dopamine release] does," said Dr. Koek, "is kind of *imprint* in these circuits the 'rewardingness' of a particular rewarding experience and kind of make a memory for the visual, auditory, tactile, gustatory, and sensory experiences that are associated with getting that rewarding feeling, and also the behaviors required to obtain that reward."

To clarify: the brain has two parts, the reasoning part (relevant portions of the prefrontal cortex) and the feeling part (the reward system, which was just described above). It is this feeling part of the reward system that helps us define what we like or don't like, even on a small level. There are millions of preferences built up in our brains throughout our lives by this reward system, one for everything we like or dislike: we like popcorn; we don't like broccoli; we like the beach but we don't like the mountains.

These "circuits" that are built in our brain throughout our lives help define the unique people we are. All of these preferences that make us unique are built up during our lives by the release of dopamine in the brain. Not only does the brain remember what gives us pleasure, it remembers the events, processes, and activities it took to get those things.

The brain remembers what gives us pleasure and the events, processes, and activities it took to get those things.

"As we go through life, we pursue rewards," said Dr. Koek. "We experience different things as rewarding and other things as less rewarding, and so we learn to kind of choose among those rewards and file among those and we actually build the [brain] circuitry stronger. . . . If you think of the neurons [in the brain] like trees, some of the branches get pruned and others grow and strengthen as they connect to neighboring neurons.

"Now what this dopamine system really does is that it gives out a kind of continuing, what's called a *basal secretion rate*, of dopamine, which keeps the system ready. Then when something comes into the environment, a reward that is either new or unexpected, there's a sudden surge of dopamine, *which feels good*."

At this point in the interview, Alexandra chimed in with "Wow!" to underscore the importance of Dr. Koek's point regarding the brain's rewarding something new or unexpected. "Which is why the brain loves novelty then," she said, "because [the brain] really loves anything new."

"Right," Dr. Koek said.

The Reward System and Substances of Abuse

"Now here's what happens with substances of abuse," continued Dr. Koek. "The classic substances would be cocaine or methamphetamine, which cause, directly, via their chemical effects, a huge surge in dopamine in this system, like *ten times* the intensity of that produced by any natural reward. And so it feels like, 'Wow, this is a reward that I've *really* got to learn about and stick to!'

"When you repeat that, eventually all of the circuits that we have with respect to knowing where to obtain and how to obtain and obtaining and pursuing and using that substance that produces that great reward, those tend to get strengthened so much that they basically *usurp*, or dramatically overshadow, all of the other reward pursuing circuits. And so that's why you end up kind of not being interested in enjoying anything else [other than the drug]. It has been said that 'the addict becomes addicted to being addicted.'"

At this point, we were naturally curious to know whether or not pornography could be considered similar to these other substances of abuse Dr. Koek was referring to, like cocaine or methamphetamine.

"As I said," Dr. Koek answered, "some people have used the term 'natural addictions' as opposed to 'chemical dependency' as representing two different categories that can both end in an addictive behavior cycle or the behavioral part of addiction. And others would say that those two form one category with the different specific choice varying with the individual and often overlapping.

"Arguments that the 'natural addictions'—and we'll just say like compulsive internet pornography use and pathological gambling—*are* basically the same as substances of abuse, [is] that in people with compulsive gambling or compulsive internet sex addiction there is a higher frequency of addiction to other drugs, to other addictive substances than there is in the general population and vice versa."

It was here that Alexandra's vast clinical experience was valuable in linking the behaviors of drug addicts with the behaviors of compulsive pornography users to say that pornography is not just *like* a substance of abuse, it *is* a substance of abuse.

"My understanding," she said, "is that when you do something where there's any kind of repetition, like constantly looking at these pornographic images, which is jacking up the neurochemistry in a certain way, the user's neuronal networks have started to fire together and, when they fire together, they wire together quite tenaciously.

"I'll have clients who are sober from pornography for say thirty, sixty days, and they keep running these pornographic images in their heads, and I think it's because the neuronal networks are so tenacious that they're making associations constantly. And over time, by my clients' not doing that, noticing they're doing it, stopping the thoughts, in six or nine months they'll say, 'You know what, I don't even think about it nearly as much anymore. It doesn't pop into my head like it used to.'"

> *The neuronal networks are so tenacious that they're making associations constantly.*

"Well, that's very similar to what happens in people who get addicted to chemicals," added Dr. Koek.

"Yeah, it's like a 'rut' in the brain is how I imagine it," concluded Alexandra.

Turning to Substances of Abuse

Often men turn to pornography when they feel stressed, upset, or unhappy. Well, now that we understand that viewing pornography releases dopamine, a neurochemical that gives us an intense euphoric rush, it only makes sense that when we feel down or frustrated, we turn to something that makes us feel good, if only momentarily. While there are obvious reasons for this, there are also some deeper, more complicated physiological reasons as well.

Dr. Koek pointed out that certain neurochemicals that are released into the body during times of stress, such as epinephrine and norepinephrine (adrenaline) and the hormone cortisol or corticosteroids, cause an indirect synergistic effect on dopamine release. What this means is that when these neurochemicals or hormones are released during times of stress, you get an easier and bigger surge of dopamine for a given new reward. Dr. Koek suggested that this is the reason addicts are much more prone to relapse, or return to their substance of abuse, when they come under stress.

But once we've turned to pornography as an opiate, those same feelings we were trying to get rid of by using pornography (frustration, shame, failure) are often re-created by using pornography. This reality is not just formed out of our psychological experience but also because of deeper, more complicated physiological reasons.

During sexual arousal and orgasm, a number of hormones and neurochemicals other than dopamine are released in the brain. With pornography use in particular, especially internet pornography use, these include testosterone (causing aggression), endorphins (producing morphinelike calmness), epinephrine and norepinephrine (discussed above), oxytocin (sensations of love), and serotonin (rest and satisfaction). This surge of so many different hormones and neurochemicals—and their relative effects on our mood—can cause a complicated and wide array of behavior.

"What I'm seeing right now is that this is really complicated and it's hard to generalize because not all cybersex addicts are created equal," said Alexandra. "You can line up ten different people who look at porn on the internet compulsively and have ten different stories as to why. One of the stories is, you know, someone who gets stressed out and the HPA axis gets activated." (What Alexandra is referring to is the hypothalamic-pituitary-adrenal axis, which is one of the main pathways through which mammals respond to stress.)

"And when that happens they run to the computer, they want to masturbate to porn to make themselves *feel* better," Alexandra continued. "In the book *Facing the Shadow*, Dr.

Patrick J. Carnes talks about 'eroticized rage,' that addicts, because they don't know how to get their needs met, can be at work and their boss pisses them off or they get into an argument with their wife at home and they start to feel like they deserve to do something good for themselves, they deserve a reward because they're so internally dysregulated. The only way they know how to regulate their nervous system is to act out sexually or engage sexually."

Again Alexandra stressed the fact that there is no way to generalize the specific reasons men turn to looking at pornography, especially given the complicated range of preferences men build up in their brains during a lifetime *and* the variety of neurochemicals that are released in the brain during sexual arousal and orgasm. But one thing that seems pretty clear is that using pornography is a coping mechanism, a way of dealing with and masking unfamiliar or unwanted emotions— essentially, a way to hide.

Using pornography is a coping mechanism— essentially, a way to hide.

"I have a guy right now who is a dyed-in-the-wool cybersex addict," said Alexandra. "He found out about phone sex when he was a teenager and he made a call one time and he was 'off to the races' ever since. He's now in his midthirties. And he's just a crazy cybersex addict, does not hire prostitutes or go to strip clubs, but when he gets anxious—and when he talks, he's got pressured speech; he smiles chronically; he can't get in touch with his feelings and has no sense of his own anger, upset, or entitlement to getting his needs met—everything is about masturbation to porn. So if he's happy, he goes to porn. If he's sad, he goes to porn. Anything—porn. Because he doesn't know how to be relational or how to engage in any other way in order to settle himself down.

"I guess my point here is that everybody is so different but what Dr. Koek was saying makes sense that when people are under stress and they have used their bodies, they've used masturbation, as a way to make the stress go away, they will turn to that coping mechanism over and over and over again. And when Dr. Koek says it's tied to the dopamine system in that way, that makes good sense to me."

From birth to the early twenties, the human brain is developing. During this time it is forming those neurological pathways Dr. Koek was talking about that help us develop the particular preferences that make us unique individuals (in other words, our brain's reward system). We like rock and roll but hate classical music, or we like cake but don't like pie. What is significant regarding the developing brain in terms of addictions is how destructive the introduction of substances of abuse can be to someone whose brain is young and in the process of developing.

Dr. Koek pointed out that based on chemical dependency literature, every year that a teenager is kept from his or her first exposure to a drug, like marijuana or alcohol, there is a 5 percent reduction, *per year*, in the risk of long-term addiction. While there have been no direct studies regarding the effects of early exposure to pornography (which we've seen is the case for *many, many* men), it can be assumed that early exposure to pornography can wire the brain in a very aggressive way to becoming addicted to pornography at an older age.

> *Early exposure to pornography can wire the brain in a very aggressive way.*

"When people are tampered with sexually before their brains are fully formed, especially when they're under ten, it's so egregious because of what it does to the brain and the body," said Alexandra. "I have a client right now whose brother was undoubtedly a sex addict and he had *bags* of pornography in his room. The brother would travel for work and be gone for stretches of time, and his mother would let the boy play in the brother's room but tell him that he 'should not get into anything he shouldn't.' We have to assume that she knew it was there but looked the other way. He began looking at the porn from a very young age.

"So very early on, he was masturbating and then he learned to ejaculate with the masturbation, and his brain is so attached to those images, making it hard to be relational with a live woman, and that becomes quite painful. That's what I call 'environmental sexual abuse,' when pornography floats around or when kids hear their parents having sex at ages when their brains can't really make sense of what's going on."

Tolerance

As both Alexandra and Dr. Koek stated, the brain loves new things. When you experience new things, your brain wants to remember them, and it does that by releasing a surge of dopamine that both helps wire its circuitry and makes you feel good so that you will repeat the activity. But once that thing or activity is no longer new, your brain releases less dopamine when it comes in contact with it. To get the same or increased dopamine high from an activity, like viewing pornography, your brain is going to look for increasingly novel forms of it.

As a psychiatrist with only a little clinical experience with sex addiction, Dr. Koek was curious to know from Alexandra if many of her clients who are internet sex addicts have reported a relative loss of interest in sex with their partners, or even a decreased enjoyment of sex relative to looking at pornography. She said, "Yes," but had more to add.

"What we also see is a tolerance, meaning what used to be arousing is no longer. So if someone used to look at heterosexual porn, now all of the sudden they're looking at group sex images, and in a matter of time they might start looking at more 'kinky,' 'out-there' configurations, which can have people looking at child pornography," she said, adding, "not because they would *ever*, *ever* touch a child but because the arousal is so great."

"It's a tolerance issue," underscored Dr. Koek.

"Because of the tolerance," agreed Alexandra. "If I took a Valium, I'd pass out. But if I took it all of the time, over time I'd probably need two, and over more time I would need three to get the same kind of relaxed effect. So we do see tolerance with people who are looking at pornography over time, and it definitely dulls their desire for sex with another human being.

"But I want to be careful there because, if you take an average guy who has no addictive tendencies and he watches soft-core porn two or three times a month on Showtime and he masturbates to that, it doesn't mean that now all of the sudden he'll be looking for hard-core or he's going to be looking for more, more, more. However, if somebody is *already* looking at porn on the internet and it's becoming problematic, there is a chance that he will develop a tolerance to it and spend more time on it or start to look at different images that he would never have dreamed of looking at before."

Environmental Cues

Once the brain has been repeatedly exposed to pornography, it not only becomes increasingly tolerant to less novel forms of it, but it also becomes attached, as Dr. Koek mentioned, "to knowing where to obtain and how to obtain and obtaining and pursuing and using." Your brain's reward system makes a connection between certain things in your personal environment that aid you in acquiring the thing that gives you that dopamine rush your reward system craves.

In the case of pornography, the simple exposure to the events or objects that have led you to or helped you acquire pornography—like feelings of loneliness, stress, or anger; the sight of your personal computer; or knowing that you will be left alone for a few hours—just those events or objects trigger a release of dopamine that activates your brain's reward system; slows your prefrontal cortex (the reasoning part of the brain); and causes you to want to acquire pornography, view it, and then possibly bring that experience to completion through masturbation and orgasm.

While Dr. Koek emphasizes the fact that we don't have the science or neuroimaging data to prove that environmental cues can cause pornography addicts in particular to want to obtain and use pornography, he does stress the similarity in behavior between pornography addicts and drug addicts, the latter group having been tested heavily in this area. "What we do know is that images of the substance or even cues like the places where the substances are obtained *do* still cause a big dopamine surge even though the substance itself does not," said Dr. Koek. "That's why I talk about being 'addicted to being addicted.'"

We get sex addicts to make sobriety plans.

Through her own clinical experience, Alexandra was quick to reinforce Dr. Koek's observations regarding addicts and environmental cues. "We get sex addicts to make sobriety plans. If they hired prostitutes on certain streets, they cannot go down those streets," she said. "There are certain newsstands people can't go by; any area where there's a strip club and they know it. I mean, people start to have a visceral response; they start reporting things like rapid heartbeats, sweaty palms. They start to have a physiological response and they talk about getting triggered all the time."

"I'll add one more comment," interjected Dr. Koek. "Again I'm speaking about what's now known in terms of brain circuitry with chemical addictions, but what we discover is that there is a kind of a neuroadaptational rewiring, such that the cues to the addictive substance kind of weigh more heavily in the balance of circuits."

Essentially, once your brain is "wired" to wanting, seeking, obtaining, and using a particular substance of abuse, those neuroadaptational changes "tend to be more permanent or lasting," as Dr. Koek has said. "Which might be what underlies this fact that 'once addicted, you're always addicted' in terms of even if you haven't used alcohol for years, it would just take one drink and it's all over."

Dr. Koek was curious to know from Alexandra's clinical perspective if she witnesses this same ease and tendency to relapse in her patients who are struggling with compulsive pornography use. Her reply was a confident yes. She also quickly pointed out that men who struggle with addictions to pornography have the deck stacked against them by our culture. Sex is everywhere—commercials, billboards, TV, computers, fashion. Alexandra jokes with her clients that if they can get sexually sober in Los Angeles, where her practice is based, they can do it anywhere.

Sex is everywhere—commercials, billboards, TV, computers, fashion.

"With alcohol, either you drink or you don't. With sexual compulsivity, it's different," Alexandra added. "And people will play tricks. They'll say, 'Well, you know, I got online and I get to the MSN home page and there's Christina Aguilera in a pair of hot pants.' And so it's *right there* and they'll click on it and say, 'I only looked for a minute!'"

Can the Brain Recover?

We know that pornography is destructive to the human soul, but what emerges from this discussion is that it can also be destructive to the human brain. Pornography stimulates the brain in ways similar to how drugs stimulate the brain; it can rewire it and change it and cause it to get out of balance. The question then becomes: can we repair the brain once we have continually exposed it to pornography?

"Once again we don't know about compulsive pornography use, but in chemical addictions what we know is that there *is* rewiring that occurs in the brain once addicts become sober," said Dr. Koek. "In fact, beginning very soon after amphetamine, cocaine, or alcohol addicts stop using, there are changes in metabolism, and within a month after cessation of alcohol use, there's evidence of regrowth of brain matter, neurons and glia, in critical brain regions, including the prefrontal region, which is involved in sort of modulating, controlling, and inhibiting behavior."

Alexandra was curious to know how long that might take. "Well, so far studies have shown there's evidence that it is already starting to occur and significantly occurring within a month after alcohol has stopped," replied Dr. Koek.

"This is curious to me," said Alexandra, "because when I see people after they've stopped these behaviors with internet pornography, within thirty days you're looking at a different person. You know, initially they feel depressed; they look like they have attention deficit problems; they look sociopathic because they've been lying like crazy and compartmentalizing. And yet after thirty days people report feeling less depressed and less shame; they actually *look* different. In Alcoholics Anonymous' *Big Book*, it says it takes ninety days to build a new character. And I believe probably it takes ninety days to build these new dendrite [neuronal] centers."

But can the brain return to what it was *before* it was exposed to pornography?

"Well, once again," added Dr. Koek, "I can't speak about pornography, but with respect to drug addiction I think it's most fair to say that some circuitry *can* rewire itself back to normal, that what you *do* makes a difference, and also, both the duration and dose of drug use make a huge difference in the potential degree of recovery. But, for example in the case of alcohol or methamphetamine addiction, immediately after stopping, addicts have severe neuropsychological deficits, deficits in memory, working memory, and visual-spatial function, and what's called executive function (behavior and social interaction). When studied as short as six months later—I don't think longer studies have been done—but three to six months later there can be normalization."

So will someone who is addicted to pornography always struggle?

"I think it's different for everybody," responded Alexandra to this question. "I can't say yes or no on that. I mean, I've seen people who really just go all the way. They recognized that this is not just about stopping their sexual behavior; it's about a lifestyle change. It's about looking at their relationships across the board and what meaning life has to them and who they are, and they just keep going and growing and never look back.

"Then other people go in fits and starts, meaning they struggle and they can't put any sober time together. Again I think it really depends on the person's level of pathology to begin with, if they're also depressed, anxious, or have trauma in their backgrounds. It's just so individual, depending on the person. Some people struggle more than others."

What to Expect When Recovering

A wonderful phrase in many substance abuse treatment programs, including Alcoholics Anonymous, is that during recovery, "You are right where you need to be." During all of the discomfort that comes along with removing a substance of abuse from your life, the feelings you have you're supposed to have. Discomfort and withdrawal are normal and good— you are right where you need to be.

Often turning to pornography is an act of masking or coping with unwanted emotions. When you stop using pornography, you'll face emotions you've been avoiding or ignoring, and you'll have to tend to them without the "aid" of pornography. In addition to this psychological response to withdrawal, there will be the physiological response—actual changes in brain chemistry that will affect your mood. Remember, if you have been using pornography extensively for years, you have changed the "wiring" of your brain. Rewiring the brain back to normal will have its own side effects.

Rewiring the brain back to normal will have its own side effects.

Dr. Koek had mentioned that problems with memory, learning, and visuospatial function might develop with long-term substance abuse. These may persist and become noticeable to the addict during the early stages of recovery. What other symptoms might a man experience during the thirty to ninety days it takes to re-regulate his behavior and brain's reward system after stopping the use of pornography?

"Well, I think what we see is anxiety, because, again, people are used to soothing themselves by way of orgasm and you're taking that away," said Alexandra. "You can see depression, irritability. People talk about starting to have feelings they've never felt before and really being kind of phobic about their affective states, which is why they got involved in the behaviors to begin with. Oftentimes sex addicts don't know how to express their feelings and/or are afraid to.

"So when you take the compulsive sexual behaviors away and you get someone to begin to be more relational, they have to start confronting their friends and family members by asking for what they want and need, being afraid they're not going to get that, tolerating disappointment and possible rejection. If they have more anxiety, they can report sleep disturbances, loss of appetite, depression, and other uncomfortable states. But typically those symptoms begin to diminish in thirty to sixty days.

"Of course by sixty days, ninety days, it starts to get really hard because then they have to stay disciplined, focused, and concentrate on their recovery. People have to stay focused so we give them a lot of assignments to engage the prefrontal cortex, to make them think, to have critical thinking—sort of like exercises for the brain. Then their intuition and insight start to appear, good judgment starts to reappear, but it requires lots and lots of focus. That's why going to 12-step meetings, working a 12-step program, getting together in groups—which is relational—are important because all of those things help socialize people and get them out of the isolation of their porn addiction."

Is Something Morally Wrong with the Porn Addict?

There is a pervasive belief in our society that for a man to have become addicted to anything, especially pornography, he must have some weakness or a morally deficient character. Many men are afraid to admit that they have challenges with pornography for fear they will be judged or ridiculed.

What would a psychiatrist or seasoned sex therapist have to say about this? Is it totally a man's fault for having become addicted, or are there other reasons this could have happened to him outside of his own free will?

"Well, this is our culture today where many messages we get say, 'You shouldn't have sex before you get married,' and 'It's a sin,' or 'You should remain abstinent,' and yet every other message says, 'Have sex!'" emphasized Alexandra.

"It's quite contradictory, right?" agreed Dr. Koek.

"Right," Alexandra continued, "and that you should be ready for sex at any place, anywhere, anytime. I mean, every ad—car ads, deodorant ads—are all selling sex all the time. It's very, very confusing. But I think, based on what we're talking about here today, there's some real neurobiological processes in effect so it doesn't make the person a bad person or they don't have enough willpower or they're not *praying* hard enough. It means they're struggling in ways they don't understand. But through a good recovery process, and a willingness to stop, they can recover their lives and their sexuality."

"One way to understand the question," said Dr. Koek, "is whether one has *become* an internet porn addict *because* one has a deficient moral character, right? And I think that, again, speaking from the chemical addictions perspective, which I have, that's definitely not the case. There are a lot of factors that determine whether one person gets addicted or, as Alexandra said, *how* one gets addicted; it's certainly not a simple question of morality like that. In fact it's also possible that addiction causes problems with one's moral character, rather than the other way around.

> *Through a good recovery process they can recover their lives and their sexuality.*

"The other thing is, as we've been saying, it seems like internet sex addiction is very similar to other addictions . . . once you get hooked, your brain circuitry gets usurped and that's not a moral, you know, thing, at least with chemical dependency, and it sounds like some of the behaviors that occur in internet sex addiction are similar."

"Right," concluded Alexandra. "You hear people in the sex addiction field talk about the 'hijacked brain.' But I like what you said about the *usurped* reward system."

Be Patient, Dear Reader

Admittedly, this chapter dropped quite a bit of information on you. Don't sweat it. The rest of this book will help you make sense out of this information and apply it to your recovery.

But if this chapter piqued your curiosity, reread it. In fact maybe give it a few weeks or months before rereading it, especially if you are sober during that time. You'll be surprised at how many new perspectives and ideas you may glean from it.

But again, be patient. Understanding all of this takes time. It will all make more sense as you move away from your addiction. Below is a suggested schedule for following up on rereading this chapter.

✓ *I have completed first reading on* _____ *(date).*

✓ *I have completed second reading one month after being sober on* _____ *(date).*

✓ *I have completed third reading three months after being sober on* _____ *(date).*

4

It's Not What You Think

Defining Normal Sexuality

> Only if we are particularly psychologically insightful or have the benefit of therapy can most of us consciously appreciate the extent to which our present experience of the world repeats our past.
>
> Dr. Michael J. Bader, *Arousal: The Secret Logic of Sexual Fantasies*

Men turn to pornography for many reasons. They could be trying to find satisfaction in something that doesn't require relationship building, or they're looking for a distraction, an opiate, to hide or mask feelings and emotions that are just too difficult or painful to face. Perhaps they were exposed to pornography early in life, wiring the circuitry of the brain in such a way that it craves pornography in adulthood.

Whatever the reason, the men who have turned to pornography have avoided for a period of time the work necessary to build a healthy sex life, and they have changed the chemistry of their brain so that achieving a healthy sex life—which might have been a difficult process anyway—has become an even more awkward and confusing prospect. In short, a sex addict simply doesn't feel the way he would normally feel.

Implement a plan to starve the addiction by staying within God's boundaries.

The only way we can start getting back on track once our brain and sexuality have been hijacked by pornography is by defining "normal" sexuality. Once we understand what God expects of us in the area of sexuality—what is okay and what is not okay and why—we can implement a plan to starve the addiction by staying within God's boundaries.

The Purpose of Sex for Christians

It's easy to give a laundry list of biblical dos and don'ts. We could point to Scripture to illustrate that God created man and woman to be united with each other only in marriage (Gen. 2:24), that adultery is against the Ten Commandments (Exod. 20:14), and that even to look at another woman with lust in the eyes is sin (Matt. 5:28). We could discuss scriptural passages, such as 1 Corinthians 6:13 that says, "The body is not meant for sexual immorality, but for the Lord, and the Lord for the body." We could pound our Bibles and shake our fists, telling each and every one of you who are struggling with your sexuality that, if you do not repent and change your behavior, you will go to hell.

We could do all of this, but not only would it be useless in helping you become sexually sober, it simply wouldn't even be scripturally accurate. In Romans 7, Paul points out that, sure, God's law—which includes prohibitions against adultery and, of course, many other things—is good. There is nothing wrong with the law, but the truth is, sin wouldn't even exist if it weren't for the law, for if the law didn't exist, there would be nothing to sin against. In other words, God's laws are good and life-giving, but those very laws create the sin against which we find ourselves struggling so fervently.

So what are we supposed to do? We know the law is good and produces life, and we know we should obey it, but sometimes it feels as if we are trying to cram our very unique selves, our very unique challenges, and our very unique (and complex) desires into a perfect Jell-O mold (law) in which we simply cannot fit!

Well, as Paul points out, not only does this cramming process not work, it in fact leads to more sin because we grow frustrated at not being able to live up to the law

Sometimes it feels as if we are trying to cram our very unique selves into a perfect Jell-O mold.

and the more frustrated we become, the more we act out. The more we act out in sin, the more distant we feel from God until, quite possibly, we give up on God altogether and give ourselves completely over to sin, pain, and destruction.

One man in the X3LA Recovery Group, a cinematographer and editor, a man who was raised in the church and who went to Christian schools throughout his childhood and college, was so frustrated with his behavior with using pornography that he considered completely throwing in the towel of his faith and producing his own porn videos for sale. He had the video equipment, editing tools, and talent. "Why not?" he thought. "If you can't beat 'em, join 'em."

Of course Paul didn't have these exact same thoughts, but he did ask the same question this man asked himself: "Who will rescue me from this body of death?" (Rom. 7:24). Paul's answer, which shouldn't come as a big surprise, was Jesus Christ.

But what the heck does that really mean? How can Jesus Christ be our "rescuer"? For starters, it doesn't mean we continue trying to cram ourselves into that Jell-O mold. Face it right now: you're never going to be able to make yourself fit, especially on your own.

And get this: Jesus doesn't even want you to.

Eric's Story

Eric's story is like that of many other men who struggle with sexual addiction. He told himself he didn't want to use pornography anymore because he knew it was not right and God didn't want him to use it. So he went a few days without using and he was proud of himself. And then he talked to his mother on the phone. They got into a fight; she belittled him, and after Eric hung up, he felt worthless, useless, and lonely.

Eric wanted to turn to what he had always turned to in these moments to make himself feel better. He wanted to pop in a porn video or watch something explicit online, but he knew that God didn't want him to and that it was a sin. So he tried to distract himself by going on a walk. But later that night, unable to sleep, he decided to surf the internet. A risqué YouTube video caught his eye, so he clicked on it, thinking, *Oh, I'll be able to stop at this one.* That video led to many others, each one more risqué than the last. Eventually Eric was watching hard-core pornography on his TV (all night) and then masturbating.

After this binge, Eric felt terrible. He felt guilty. He felt worthless, abominable, and a sinner against God. With the early morning light creeping through his window, he got down on his hands and knees and prayed to God for forgiveness. He asked God to accept him. He told him he was sorry. Eric promised God that he'd never do it again.

Do you know what Paul would say to Eric if he saw him on his hands and knees praying for forgiveness? First of all, he would ask Eric if he were a Christian and if he had confessed with his mouth "Jesus is Lord" and believed in his heart that

"God raised him from the dead" (Rom. 10:9). When Eric said yes, Paul would have looked him kindly in the eyes and said, "Then why are you asking for something you already have?"

Please take a second to think this question through, because it is more than just a rhetorical tool used to get us to another point. This *is* the point. In fact, this question serves as the crux of this book's discussion. It is the linchpin on which sexual addiction hinges. It is the question that leads to the answer that all sexually addicted men are longing to hear.

Why are we asking for something we already have?

We ask for something we already have because we don't totally get the reality that God is no longer condemning us because of our behavior. Through Christ, we are redeemed, justified freely by God's grace (Rom. 3:23–24). What God accomplished through his Son was complete and total forgiveness for anything we have done or will do. Our behavior, whether or not it involves pornography or sex or strip clubs, is not what God is interested in. He wants our heart.

So prayer, in this context, is not for God; it is for the believer. It is an opportunity to give God—not pornography, not sex, not money—his proper place in your life. It is an opportunity to become centered and refocused. If God has your heart—if you feel loved, and cared for, and joyful—you simply will not want to do the things that you once did. You won't want to turn to the false gods of pornography, anonymous sex, or strip clubs to feel loved, cared for, and joyful. You will be, as Paul says in Philippians 4:12, "content in any and every situation."

Why are we asking for something we already have?

Sounds Good But . . .

Many men we have worked with, when they hear us proclaim God's love through Jesus Christ as the pathway to recovery, think, *Great, so what you're telling me is that God is no longer condemning me for my behavior, but since I continue to be addicted to pornography, it must be because I'm incapable of feeling Christ's love. Now I feel worse than before. What's wrong with me?*

Well, nothing is wrong with you. But what we must understand about ourselves, and our ability to feel God's love, is that there are a number of layers, accumulated throughout our lives, between who we are in the world and the kingdom of God that is within us (Luke 17:21). We don't feel God's calming presence because too many thoughts, emotions, and feelings have come between God and us. We've accumulated some of these thoughts, emotions, and feelings through the course of long, troubling lives filled with pornography, strip clubs, prostitutes, numerous anonymous sexual partners, distracting music, hours of watching TV, overwork, unhealthy relationships—the list goes on.

But the biggest layer that has accumulated, the layer that happens to be at the core of sexual addiction, is the layer that was built when we were young, when we were children, when we were least in control of our lives and who we were capable of becoming.

A tall, handsome, sociable, and highly intelligent young man named Zander first started coming to the X3LA Recovery Group after five years of wild living. He had come to LA from the East Coast to work as a cinematographer, editor, and, eventually, a writer. Living near the Sunset Strip in West Hollywood and working at a hip and trendy hotel, Zander was given access to just about any substance of abuse he could dream of. Numerous women were available to him and, of course, there was pornography.

Zander was sick and tired of the self-destructive life he was living. Though not raised as a Christian, he knew about the Christian life and had a sense of what was right and wrong. Many of his friends, who partied and had sex with their girlfriends, called themselves Christians.

Right before he started attending X3LA, Zander hit rock bottom; his relationships with both men and women were about nothing more than finding meaning in sex, lots of pornography, and alcohol. He was, as he reported, "crushed to the depths of his soul" by depression and loneliness. He wanted something meaningful and real.

Unlike many others, Zander came to our group with a great deal of self-determination and good intentions. He was going to stop using frequent sex with women and pornography as a way to find meaning in life. He was simply going to stop it. But when he changed his lifestyle cold turkey, he found that it wasn't as easy as he had hoped. He struggled with the physiological aspects of recovery, such as retraining his brain to want healthy stimuli (exercise or conversation) instead of unhealthy stimuli (anonymous sex and pornography), but there was something else that was making it difficult for him to stay on track, some feeling, some profound sense of internal emotional discomfort that wasn't necessarily new but certainly was laid bare by his abstinence.

Some profound sense of internal emotional discomfort was laid bare by his abstinence.

One long summer afternoon, Zander came to my (Steven's) office to talk. He was severely troubled by the emotions he was feeling and was desperate to overcome this "body of death," as Paul would call it. Zander and I talked about how his life was going in West Hollywood, how work was, and how his relationship with God was progressing. All seemed to be relatively fine.

Then I asked him about his relationship with his parents and family. He let out a sigh and told me that he and his mother were in pretty good standing and enjoyed talking frequently. He also had a good relationship with his sisters, but with his father things were a little bit more complicated.

His father had divorced his mother when Zander was thirteen. Zander and his father had a contentious relationship—not because of Zander's behavior but because his father is a stubborn man who has very strong opinions about life and living, and Zander, essentially a good-hearted, willing-to-please young man, wasn't going to disagree with him.

Zander's father's beliefs are right out of the *Great American Macho Playbook* (if there were such a thing). In his mind, men are not to communicate feelings, and a man is expected to have sex with his girlfriend. Most important, men are to "conquer" as many women as they can possibly conquer. In fact Zander's father showed the most interest in his son's life when Zander discussed his female relationships.

Zander's father, unlike the rest of the family, is wholly disinterested in Christianity and faith. In fact it was Christianity that had caused the greatest rupture between Zander's mother and father.

When I asked about his father, there was a palpable tension in the room. It was clear that their relationship was a troubling one. His father did not approve of his returning to church. They had argued about it over the phone. In short, Zander was living a life that was completely opposite to how his father lived and was afraid to admit that to him.

"What if you told him about your new life?" I had asked Zander. "What if you discussed your faith and your new life of celibacy?"

He laughed as if the mere thought of doing so would be like taking a lit match to a tank of gasoline.

Fortunately, Zander is, as I said, a very intelligent young man, willing to imagine the other side of possibilities. He thought for a second and then said, "I don't know. I've never considered that before."

"Do you think," I asked, "that if you were somehow able to be honest with your father, to let him know where you stand on your faith, on your sexual health, and on your desire to be sexually pure despite what your father may do or say or think, that you would feel some sense of relief from these feelings of discomfort that you have about yourself, these feelings that often make you want to act out sexually?"

Zander continued to smile, but this time it was more of a smile of realization, not bemusement. "I don't know," he said, continuing to smile. "I don't know."

It was clear that Zander was starting to put his finger on what it was that was making him feel so compelled to act out with women and with porn. His relationship with his father made him feel that there was something wrong with him, at his core, if he were to live his life any differently from how his father lived. If he were to be honest with his father, he believed his father would probably do to him what he had done to his sisters and mother: cut him off, stop talking to him, essentially disown him.

Zander's sexual addiction had very little to do with sex.

Zander was faced with the very real possibility that for him to achieve his sexual sobriety, he had to journey down that same road that Paul had to journey down. He would need to learn how to be "content in any and every situation" (Phil. 4:12), even if those situations included being honest with his father, or at least setting boundaries on when and how often he communicated with him, despite what his father might say or do. In other words, Zander's sexual addiction had very little to do with sex and everything to do with wanting to mask the icky feelings his father caused, feelings that made him feel wrong, bad, or stupid. To pursue the life he knew Christ wanted him to live, he might have to experience what Mark 10:29–31 speaks of: "No one who has left home or brothers or sisters or mother or father or children or fields for me and the gospel will fail to receive a hundred times as much in this present age . . . and in the age to come, eternal life."

A Deeper Perspective

Not everyone has a story like Zander's, of course. Every man is unique, with particular struggles and challenges that may or may not be related to his father. Unpleasant feelings can result from any number of relationships—with a mother, siblings, grandparents, coaches, or even nannies.

The truth is, for the majority of men who are struggling with sexual addiction, the cause of the addiction is the existence of some "hardwired" emotions that broadcast that there is something wrong with them. If these hardwired emotions say you are bad or stupid or dumb or ugly or fat, you are going to approach the world with very different behavior from someone who was hardwired to believe he is good, smart, wise, handsome, or physically healthy.

Someone who believes at his very core that he is worthwhile and important will most assuredly not feel compelled to drive into a shady part of the city to take advantage of a poor young woman for sex; instead, he might help women like her get off the streets and into safe, loving communities. A man who feels valueless and insignificant at his very core will want, if possible, to get rid of those feelings of worthlessness, if only for a moment. Hence, we end up with men who use pornography, strip clubs, prostitutes, and compulsive masturbation because it makes them feel good.

> *"Hardwired" emotions broadcast that there is something wrong with them.*

This is a big topic, to be sure. But there are some "starter principles" that will help us get to the core of why men act out sexually. These starter principles come from the world of psychoanalysis, a branch of mental health that explores life experiences, *especially* early childhood, to discover why we behave the way we behave. After we present these principles, it will be your job to continue to explore your own inner life through counseling, small group participation, or private journaling. This work will not only help you discover where your core emotions came from, but will also help you learn how to manage those core emotions in ways that lead you to contentment not self-destruction.

Basics of Psychoanalysis

In his book *Arousal: The Secret Logic of Sexual Fantasies*, Michael J. Bader offers a wonderful summary of the core concepts of psychoanalysis, especially as they relate to sex and sexuality.[2]

Beginning with a child's relationship with his parents or caregivers, Bader stresses that since birth we are significantly drawn and attached to our primary caregivers, especially our parents (if they are around). Our very survival, both emotionally and physically, is under their control. They feed us, clothe us, shelter us, and nurture us. In this relationship, there is a very honored "primacy" given to our caregivers. They are, excuse the comparison, gods, for our very existence and being depend on them.

In this relationship, we are very acutely attuned to our parents' or caregivers' moods. If they are happy, we are happy, because it means that the source from which we receive all of our physical and emotional well-being is strong and maintained. If they are depressed, upset, or angry, we feel even worse than depressed, upset, or angry; we feel as if we might not get our needs met. In feeling as if we might not get our needs met, we change the situation we are in to work in our favor. Well, how can a small, powerless child change the situation he is in to work in his favor? As Dr. Bader points out, he does so *by changing himself*.

Pathogenic Beliefs

To maintain their nurturing relationship with a depressed, upset, or angry parent or caregiver, children blame themselves as the *cause* of their caregiver's depression, upset, or anger. In the world of a small child, there is no ability to see, recognize, or understand that something *outside* of himself could possibly cause a parent or caregiver's dark moods. In essence, if a parent or caregiver is in a dark place, it must be the child's fault; he is, or must have done, something wrong.

The more a young child is exposed to the negative moods or abuse of a parent or caregiver, the more the child develops a negative self-image. There's simply a "bad" feeling, a sense that something is not right with him, that he is dumb or stupid or ugly or fat or whatever other negative self-beliefs he may have acquired. Bader calls these beliefs *pathogenic beliefs*, based on the work of psychoanalyst Joseph Weiss.

Repetition Compulsion

The most troubling aspect of our relationship with our parents or childhood caregivers is that throughout our lives we wish to remain psychologically connected to them. They were, at one time, the font of our existence; they were the ones who maintained our physical and emotional selves, even if, in some cases, they did it through cruelty and abuse. When adults cut themselves off *mentally* from parents or caregivers, when they deny what was said about them (good or bad), they are, essentially, losing their emotional and psychological center. Because of our desire *not* to lose our emotional and psychological center, to remain "stable" and "in our proper place," we tend to look for events or situations or people that reinforce or mirror those negative beliefs we have about ourselves. This is called *repetition compulsion*.

One can see from this how people get stuck in what most other people would consider to be unhealthy, damaging, or dangerous patterns of living. They choose abusive partners, for instance, not because they don't know any better but because unhealthy, damaging, or dangerous patterns of living reflect what they see to be their true value based on their pathogenic beliefs. It just "feels right," or "is comfortable," or "is where I belong." Generally the more severe the exposure to a depressed, neglectful, or abusive parent, the more severe the pathogenic beliefs and thus the more severe the acting out later in life, whether through drugs, alcohol, or sex (for instance).

Looking now at Zander's situation through the lens of psychoanalysis, it is much clearer why it so difficult for him to break free from his father's opinions of him, and thus break free from the negative feelings that have caused him to act out sexually. For Zander to decide that he doesn't care about what his father thinks of his decisions would be to run the risk of being cut off, both psychologically and physically, from the very person who, from day one, has been Zander's emotional and physical provider, sustainer, and ground, for better or worse. This is the reason our relationships with our parents, caregivers, and close family members are so very important and why they can be so very painful if they aren't mutually re-spectful and respecting.

Rebuild our core sense of self into the right image through God.

As we saw in Mark 10:29–31, Jesus called his followers to leave houses, brothers, sisters, mothers, fathers, children, and lands for his sake and the gospel. Jesus calls us to recognize that those imperfect people who helped to create our core selves, our very identities, are not *really* the center of the universe; they are not the Real Being who determines our self-worth. God is. Jesus is challenging us to "leave" those people who have caused us to believe negative things about ourselves; he is challenging us to break free psychologically from these individuals and rebuild our core sense of self into the right image through God, which is that we are valuable, lovable, worthy, and cherished.

In Romans 6:11 Paul goes so far as to tell us to count ourselves "dead to sin but alive to God in Christ Jesus." What he means is that we must learn to be dead, numb, and unresponsive to those people who cause us to feel "bad" or "wrong" about ourselves, and instead be alive and responsive to the glory, power, and love of God through Jesus Christ. No easy task, for sure, but one that can be accomplished if a person is willing to put in the work.

What the Bible Says

The Bible is loaded with plenty of sexual discussion: Onan (Gen. 38:9), Lot and his daughters (Gen. 19:30–38), David and Bathsheba (2 Samuel 11), the Corinthians, and others. From these stories, and the Levitical law, we could develop our own version of what is right and wrong regarding sex.

Let there be no mistake about it, this would be *our own version* of what is right and wrong. Every single Christian community from the resurrection on-down has devised their own rules—based on the Bible, mind you—of what sex is for and how it should be used: "sex is only between a man and his wife"; "sex is only between a man and his *wives*"; "sex is wrong for both men and women"; "sex is only for procreation"; "sex is to be enjoyed"; "sex is an abomination." The list goes on and on.

To devise and list a set of rules and regulations to be followed regarding sex would not only be the easy way out, it would not help you in any way achieve the freedom and sobriety you are looking for. We've said this before and we'll say it again, Jesus doesn't just want you to look good from the outside; he wants you to *feel* good from the inside because if you *feel* good from the inside, your outsides will glow with his light and glory.

Throughout the years, both of us have been asked many questions regarding what is right and wrong in terms of sex. The big questions are:

✗ Is it okay to masturbate?

✗ Is it okay to have oral sex?

✗ Is it okay for me and my fiancée to have sex before marriage if we plan on being married anyway?

✗ Is it okay to look at porn if I am married and my wife knows about it?

✗ Is it okay if my wife and I look at porn together?

✗ Is it okay if my wife and I use sexual aids?

✗ Is it okay if I masturbate to R-rated movies?

✗ Is it okay to slap my wife when we have sex?

✗ Is it okay for my wife to slap me when we have sex?

✗ Is it okay to have sexual fantasies about men but not actually have sex with them?

✗ Is it okay to have homosexual sex?

Hopefully one can see by this list of questions how absurd it would be for *anyone* to simply answer yes or no to any of these questions. Sure, we could point to Scripture to explain the reasons for answering either yes or no, but it is more important to determine *why* we do what we do. Instead of asking what is "right" and what is "wrong" regarding certain sexual practices, the better question to ask is, *Why do I want to do it?*

In other words, what feelings, emotions, or issues do you have in your life and in your heart that make you think it is a good idea to act out sexually? What negative feelings do you have inside of you that make you want to reach for the most powerful drug at your disposal?

For a man to say he wishes to abstain from masturbation because he wants to think about "whatever is true, whatever is noble, whatever is right, whatever is pure, whatever is lovely, whatever is admirable" (Phil. 4:8) makes perfect sense to Christians. For a man to say he wants to masturbate two times a day because he is so stressed out about his parents' divorce, his poor college grades, or his challenges in athletics doesn't make sense to Christians because that means he is being controlled by his "body of death" (Rom. 7:24).

For a man to say he wishes to save his virginity for marriage because he wants to experience the beauty of his future wife's body with no preconceived ideas of what beauty is makes perfect sense to Christians. For a man to say he wants to have premarital sex because he wants to prove to his friends that he's a man doesn't make perfect sense to Christians because we are called to live according to Christ's purpose not man's (Rom. 8:28).

For a man to say that he wishes to have sex with his wife because he wants to give and receive love makes perfect sense to Christians. For a man to say he wants to slap his wife while having sex because he was abused as a child and needs to feel as if he is the aggressor instead of the abused doesn't make perfect sense to Christians because we are taught to "be content whatever the circumstances" (Phil. 4:11). Content people do not hit!

As if there were such a thing as moral *porn!*

Before his first meeting at the X3LA Recovery Group, a gay man asked Steven if it was okay for him to join. "Of course it's okay," said Steven. "Why wouldn't it be?" The man reasoned that, since he engages in using "immoral porn," maybe he wouldn't be allowed.

He was making a fascinating distinction between heterosexual and homosexual pornography. As if there were such a thing as *moral* porn! But this illustrates how ridiculous it is to try to achieve sexual health by devising a biblical list of dos and don'ts. Because many churches teach that homosexuality is the premier sin of sins, instead of teaching the importance of feeling loved by God *despite* your sexual orientation, individuals get the impression that it is simply a bad habit to be a heterosexual addicted to porn but it is a *damnable abomination* to be a homosexual addicted to porn. In either case there is a man who suffers from some deep profound hurt that he is trying desperately to mask by acting out sexually. God's love, through Jesus Christ, is the preeminent cure, *not* rules.

Paul sums up this thinking in a wonderful way in Romans 8:5–6: "Those who live according to the sinful nature have their minds set on what that nature desires; but those who live in accordance with the Spirit have their minds set on what the Spirit desires. The mind of sinful man is death, but the mind controlled by the Spirit is life and peace."

Something to Think About

Dr. Bader's book *Arousal* is not simply an introduction to psychoanalysis and sex. In it he offers a fascinating theory regarding what arouses us sexually and what that may mean in understanding ourselves as individuals.

Bader's theory is that the particular fantasies or configurations that turn us on sexually—whether they are a particular type of person, in a particular situation, with pain, without pain, and so on—are not so much efforts at re-creating past situations or abuses (repetition compulsion) as much as ways in which we psychologically disable the anxiety that our pathogenic beliefs have formed in us.

Let us explain. It is Dr. Bader's contention that sexual arousal is a significant and very powerful aim of the adult human mind. The trouble is, sexual arousal cannot coexist with anxiety. So what you have in an anxious person (that is, someone with pathogenic beliefs) is a real desire to have some sort of sexual experience, but at the same time his state of anxiety keeps his sexual desire from "coming out to play." For the human mind to experience sexual arousal, it "flips the switch" of anxiety by constructing fantasies that make it okay to be sexually aroused.

A perfect example is someone who enjoys inflicting physical pain during sex. This is not because the person wants to re-create the physical abuse he experienced in childhood; instead, in a situation where he is the abuser instead of the abused, he is in a state of psychological safety (instead of anxiety) that allows him to be sexually aroused.

Think of a crooked oak tree growing up through the cracks of a broken sidewalk: it's not the oak tree's fault for wanting to grow; it's the concrete's fault for limiting the oak tree's space. What seems most tragic in this situation is that the oak tree (which represents our sexuality) and the sidewalk (which represents unhealthy family systems or oppressive societies) *both* suffer damage in this relationship. The tree is crooked because the sidewalk didn't nurture, and the sidewalk is broken because the tree is just doing what it was designed to do.

> *Think of a crooked oak tree growing up through the cracks of a broken sidewalk.*

In looking at this theory of sexual arousal, one can see again how ridiculous it is for Christians to turn immediately to rules and regulations when dealing with sexual issues. If the cause of much sexual immorality is because the person feels bad or wrong or different, making him feel bad or wrong or different because he didn't live up to rules and regulations will only make the situation worse. What is needed is love not rules.

If it was hate that created the feelings that caused a man to want to masturbate compulsively, use pornography, visit strip clubs, and hire prostitutes, then it is love and only love that will help that man stop. If you are looking for a list of biblical rules and regulations regarding sex and sexuality, there is no better one than that offered by Paul in 1 Corinthians 13:4–7: "Love is patient, love is kind. It does not envy, it does not boast, it is not proud. It is not rude, it is not self-seeking, it is not easily angered, it keeps no record of wrongs. Love does not delight in evil but rejoices with the truth. It always protects, always trusts, always hopes, always perseveres."

Our Personal Position

Our personal position regarding what is right and wrong when it comes to sex and sexual activity is that *sex and all sexual activity are to exist only within marriage and between the partners of that marriage. Period.*

Yes, this position is highly biblical. If a man pursues and feels God's love through Jesus Christ, his church, his community, his friends, his partner, and above all himself, he most certainly will not wish to engage in any sexual activity other than that with his marriage partner. Then sex becomes an act of reciprocal love, not an act of selfish hate.

We believe that those who are not married must abstain from all sexual activity, not because we wish to follow the rules and regulations handed down to us by God but because we want to honor God. Just following rules and regulations is to ignore completely Christ's saving action on the cross. Christ doesn't want us to try to follow rules and regulations, because we'll always fail at it. He came to fulfill the law. He wants us to have a close, personal relationship with him, because if we feel loved and nurtured and content, we will simply not be interested in engaging in sexual activities that spread hurt, pain, suffering, and hate.

Sex within a marriage is reciprocal, like an ecosystem, or the Trinity itself—Father, Son, and Holy Spirit. Sexual activity outside of marriage is like the dumping of toxic nuclear waste:

it goes out in rivers of radioactive sludge never to be reclaimed and always to be dealt with in human suffering and pain.

If you are participating in any sexual activities outside of marriage, you need to stop, and it is the next two chapters that will help you devise a plan to make that happen. But the real reason we abstain from sexual activity outside of marriage is not to mindlessly follow rules and regulations. We abstain so that we may face, understand, and manage the uncomfortable feelings that interfere with the peace and contentment that God offers through Jesus Christ. Anything short of that is a Band-Aid; anything short of that is counterfeit and will lead only to death.

Sex within a marriage is reciprocal.

✔ *Can you pinpoint any negative feelings (pathogenic beliefs) you have about yourself? Write them down here or in a journal.* _____

_____

_____

✔ *Can you trace those negative feelings back to a source, to a relationship in your life that feels or felt very conditional? For example, did anyone make you feel that if you behaved in a certain way, that person would love you?* _____

_____

_____

✔ *Can you think of ways in which you can manage your feelings caused by this person/people that don't include acting out sexually? Ideas may include private counseling, joining a support group, or making new friends.*

_____

_____

_____

5

A Good Plan

Starving the Addiction

Robert Bly once remarked that growing up is making your body do what it does not want to do. Most addicts have not been able to develop normally, and so the normal maturation process starts. They start to do what they say they will. And they feel good about themselves. Up until this point, they have been filled with shame and have made decisions on the basis of what people will think of them. Now they are making decisions on the basis of what is right for them. This is the turning point.

Patrick Carnes, *Facing the Shadow*

We've gone over the basics of the soul-searching a man must do when struggling with an addiction to pornography. We've pointed out the importance of admitting to yourself and others that you have this struggle, committing yourself to overcoming it, and understanding the addiction's nature. We've even defined the boundaries and ultimate destination for your sexuality: *sex and all sexual activity are to exist only within marriage and between the partners of that marriage. Period.*

Of course achieving this end by simply willing it, or even by fervent prayer, can be agonizing at best and futile at worst. Instead of trying to go from point A to point Z without any indication of how to pass through all the points in between (which will undoubtedly cause confusion and relapse), you need a measured, clear course of action.

So let's outline the points you'll need to travel through to go from *wanting* to stop looking at pornography to *actually stopping*. We call this process "starving the addiction" because, ultimately, our goal is to quite literally starve it out of our brains.

As we saw in chapter 3, looking at porn builds new neurological pathways in your brain. These pathways cause you to crave, seek, and use more pornography and at increasingly rapid rates.

> *We call this process "starving the addiction."*

Now it's time to squelch those pathways, choke them off from existence. Your goal is not only to stop using pornography but also to allow your brain to rebuild new, healthier neurological pathways that urge you to seek and enjoy healthy things, such as good friends, family, and your God-given purpose.

This won't be easy at first. It may be the most challenging thing you've undertaken in your life, but as more time passes and more progress is made, the power of this demon will diminish. In addition to this freedom, the pride, wonder, and fulfillment of a healthy sexuality will make your days bright and your evenings full of hope.

Please understand that this will be an ongoing process and it isn't going to be easy. The goal here isn't perfection or finding absolutes—it is discovering all of the little choices you make that lead to destruction and then learning to make choices that lead to health and victory. This process will not only help you eliminate pornography from your life, it will also reveal a new and wonderful person hidden deep inside of you.

Every day I (Craig) get emails from people who are struggling. So many of them talk about the fact that this is not easy.

> I am a 23 year old guy. I have struggled with online porn since I was about ten years old. Even though I have always struggled with this I didn't start to battle it until I was about 19. Over the last few years God has given me some great victories in battling this sin, but porn has continued to be a struggle in my life. Recently I moved to a new area. Now that I am away from a familiar group of supportive brothers in Christ I have slipped back into some of my old habits. I am so ashamed of this sin, and really can't even rationalize why these impulses have such control over me. This sin disgusts me, and it breaks me when I think of what price has been paid for it . . . and still I can't shake it. I just don't know what to do with it anymore.

Binary Thinking

When discussing making the choices that lead to overcoming porn, the members of the X3LA Recovery Group created the term "binary thinking." In the world of computers, the language is a series of ones and zeroes. Their many switches are either on or off.

In the same way, every time we are faced with decisions in life, we are required to say yes or no to them. "Should I get up from the couch? Yes or no? Should I eat now? Yes or no?" It's like having to turn the switches on or off.

Our goal when trying to go from wanting to stop using pornography to actually stopping—a very big yes or no—is to break down and examine all of the little decisions we make in our daily life to see what we are saying yes or no to and where all of these little decisions are taking us.

If we can find the smallest possible decisions that we make that eventually lead to the big decision of looking at pornography, and instead make different little decisions when we come to them, overcoming this addiction will become exponentially easier.

This is no different from what we discussed in chapter 1 about the muddy, slippery pit of pornography. The only way to climb from it is by using the footholds; the more footholds we give ourselves, the easier the ascension will be.

One member of the X3LA Recovery Group had a relapse. After about two months of sobriety, he fell back into the pit. When he confessed this to the group, we took the time to break down and analyze the decisions he was making that helped lead to his relapse.

We discovered that his relapse started when he was at the mall, letting his eyes and mind wander toward various women. Unfortunately, this caused in him a sexual arousal that triggered his mind and body to crave some form of sexual release. Hours later, he asked his wife to have sexual intercourse with him. For whatever reason, she refused. Feeling as if he had no outlet for his passions (if only subconsciously), he waited for his family to go to bed, took the quiet opportunity to log onto the computer, viewed porn, and brought his sexual arousal to completion.

As a support group, the X3LA men were able to take this man's experience and break it down into as many pieces as possible. In fact the details of this man's relapse only came to light *because* the group members helped him remember them; even the man himself was not quite aware of all of the little subconscious decisions he had made that day. These decisions included choosing to fantasize sexually about women in the first place, choosing to become sexually aroused, choosing not to be confessional about his mistake, choosing to see no hope beyond his wife's refusal for sex, choosing to allow himself access to his computer, and choosing pornography over any number of other stress-relieving activities.

Once the group made apparent all of the choices this man had subconsciously made (and remember, *not* to make a choice is still making a choice), they were able to help him see the other little choices he had available to him that would have prevented him from looking at pornography. These choices didn't just include avoiding looking at women at the mall and allowing himself to fantasize about them sexually. They also included choosing immediately to confess his sexual arousal to God, his account-ability partner, or even his wife; choosing to at least discuss the possibility of scheduling a time for sex with his wife to give him hope; choosing to remove his computer from reach; and ultimately choosing other positive "God-sanctioned" activities to enjoy other than pornography, including exercise, watching a movie, or simply going to bed.

The only way to climb from it is by using the footholds.

Breaking down your choices to see how you can make better ones does not always provide an easy answer. Even if this man had been aware of the many choices he could have made, he still may not have made good choices, or the choices he made may have led to other challenges (for example, recognizing that his wife is not as available sexually as he may need or even that his marriage is profoundly troubled).

But this is the point: at the core of your very being, you have to accept the new reality that using pornography is *no longer an option in managing your emotional life*, and you need to provide yourself with as many alternative choices as you can possibly think up—and then choose to actively take them. Just as the apostle Paul wrote in Romans 6:11, you must consider yourself "dead to sin but alive to God in Christ Jesus."

You are now *dead* to pornography. Accept this new reality and live it out.

Defining Your Triggers

A man does not just go from doing nothing to suddenly looking at pornography. Something happens in his environment that gets him to think that using pornography will fill some inherent need in his heart or in the neurobiology of his brain. We call this something a trigger. Your goal is to pinpoint your triggers, then change or avoid them.

There are two different types of triggers: sexual and nonsexual. The definition of a sexual trigger is pretty clear: the images, sounds, textures, tastes, or smells of a sexual object— for instance, a woman. The definition of a nonsexual trigger is anything that is not sexual in nature, like the sight of a computer, that causes you to crave something sexual.

Sexual Triggers

While sexual triggers seem obvious, they might not be. Of course, pornography is a sexual trigger, but what really *is* pornography? Definitions vary widely from culture to culture and even state to state. This is partially the reason it is so difficult to legislate against pornography.

Since pornography and sexual triggers are so specific to each individual, we've created a very simple definition: *a sexual trigger is anything that stimulates you sexually*. Any image or idea that makes you want to have some sort of sexual release (like sex or masturbation) is a sexual trigger.

There is, of course, a whole range of sexual triggers available today that fall outside of what is culturally considered pornography. These could include popular men's magazines that have photos of scantily clad women on their covers or in their pages, such as the *Sports Illustrated* swimsuit issue; R-rated movies with sex scenes; or even PG-rated movies with implied sex scenes. Taken to the extreme, if pictures of female tennis players in the sports section are causing you to become sexually aroused, at this point in your healing, you should consider those images to be sexual triggers.

Your goal is to pinpoint your triggers, then change or avoid them.

Again if something sexual in nature is causing you to become sexually aroused—and that thing may be different for everyone—then you must consider that particular thing a sexual trigger.

Nonsexual Triggers

Nonsexual triggers can be both environmental and emotional and are often more difficult to pinpoint than sexual triggers, since they are not as obvious. A good rule of thumb is that if you are becoming sexually aroused or triggered to want to look at pornography, and there appear to be no sexual triggers in sight, there is probably something within your environment or about your emotional state that is triggering your brain to want to use pornography.

The addicted brain provides you with a surge of dopamine to help you remember a substance of abuse—pornography in this case—and that dopamine surge also helps you remember the circumstances, events, locations, and tools needed to acquire that substance of abuse. In this case, sensing locations or objects that were present when you used pornography—like the sight of a computer, the smell of a room, or the presence of a certain person—could all be environmental nonsexual triggers that could cause you to relapse.

There are many emotional states that trigger pornography use—and it is your job to try to pinpoint these states so you can either work at removing them from your life or at least learn to manage them. Alcoholics Anonymous and other 12-step programs have an acrostic for the four most perilous states for people with addictions: HALT. It stands for hungry, angry, lonely, or tired. If you are feeling any of these emotional states, be on the lookout for being triggered; conversely, if you are feeling triggered to use pornography, look for any of these emotional states as the cause.

Many emotional states trigger pornography use.

The reason you may turn to using pornography when you're feeling a certain uncomfortable emotion is wrapped up in fear. Instead of facing the emotion, or working to understand why you are feeling a certain way, you may be using pornography as a coping mechanism, a way to hide from the emotional state that seems to be too big and complex to alleviate on your own.

It is important to note that nonsexual triggers aren't limited to negative feelings. Successes in life, celebrations, feelings of good cheer, and/or inclusion by friends and family can elicit emotions of happiness that may cause an addict to relapse. An addict may think, *It's been a while since I looked at pornography, why don't I just take a little peek.*

Don't do it. *This is a zero-tolerance proposition.*

There is never a reason to look at pornography, ever!

Avoiding Your Triggers

The thought of avoiding the triggers mentioned above, once you have managed to pinpoint what they are, may be as daunting as the thought of trying to stop using pornography altogether. But once again, there are smaller "binary" decisions you can make in regard to these triggers that can make your overall challenge less formidable.

Essentially, you want to create a "victorious environment" for yourself. If you want to avoid catching a cold, don't drink from the cup of a person who has a cold. If you want to triumph over this addiction, avoid your triggers. There are three major ways of accomplishing this: physically removing triggers, psychologically removing triggers, and remaining continually confessional.

For a recovering alcoholic, one little drink is all it may take for him to return to a lifestyle that leads to death. You must realize the same danger and commit yourself to sobriety. *Pornography is simply no longer an option in regulating your sexuality and/or your personal emotional states.* Like a man who has already swum halfway across a large lake and grown tired, the option of turning back is not viable. It makes more sense to keep on swimming to the other shore.

Physically Removing Triggers

The physical removal of all sexual and nonsexual triggers may be the most obvious action step you can take in overcoming your addiction, but it's also the most difficult. If you don't change how you live —your physical environment and who and what are in it—all the efforts you make to change the way you think will most likely be futile.

The physical triggers you need to remove depend on you as an individual, as everyone's life is different. But start with removing anything that is or helps you get pornography, the environment that triggers its use or allows for it, and friendships that support your use. Does this mean that you need to get rid of your computer, move from your current neighborhood, and make new friends? That answer is up to you, but if you value your sobriety, and your lifestyle is causing you to crave pornography, we recommend taking drastic steps.

Your computer is the most obvious starting point in removing physical triggers. For most men who struggle with pornography, the computer is the central lever that controls not only the addiction but their entire life.

A man who is serious about overcoming his addiction, and ultimately serious about reclaiming his life and sexuality, must take the time and soul-searching necessary to be honest and come to grips with whether this modern invention is improving his life and faith or completely destroying it.

Of course many men rely on computers for their livelihood. Getting rid of their computer, even for a season, may seem to be out of the question. This *is* a sticking point. But once again, there are some binary choices to be made here. Either you feel you can remain sober by keeping your computer or you do not. The goal here is your sobriety, *not your job*. If you feel that with some help you can keep your computer and remain sober, there are some wonderful options and tools available to help you.

If you value your sobriety, we recommend taking drastic steps.

First, you can make some social and behavioral decisions to help keep you accountable online. This includes personal rules as to when and how you will use the computer. If using the computer at night is a trigger, use it only during the day. If using the computer alone is a trigger, place it in a communal location in your house or workspace. Simply rearranging the position of your computer screen so it faces your office doorway, for instance, might be enough of a deterrent (or reminder) not to look at pornography.

More potent tools that can prevent you from looking at pornography on the computer include blocking and accountability software. Blocking software, like Safe Eyes, electronically prevents explicit sexual material from entering your computer. Accountability software, like XXXchurch's free X3watch, monitors the sites you visit and every two weeks sends email reports of any questionable websites you have visited to two accountability partners of your choosing. Needless to say, this opens the door for some rather interesting conversations.

I (Craig) get so many emails from people who are struggling when they are on the computer and/or when they are up late at night. These are two environments you can easily avoid if you are serious about moving away from sexual sin. Notice that both of these are immediately evident in this email:

> It's about 2 o'clock in the morning and I just finished up with a web cam chat. I feel like garbage! What felt so good at the moment now feels disgusting and wrong. I have been dealing with an addiction to pornography for five years now. It's been progressively getting worse—pictures to clips to movies to chatting to almost actual sex. I'm at the point where when I have a relationship with a woman i solely want sex and that's not God's purpose for a relationship. I have given this to God time and time again but have yanked it back. It used to be something i would do to escape certain stressful situations but now it's become something i do whenever i have a moment of free time.

Getting rid of, or altering, the medium through which you view pornography is just the beginning of physical removal. Personal stashes of pornography—whether in digital, analog, or print formats—*must be completely and irrevocably destroyed*. Just throwing them in the trash is not sufficient. Not only do we want to remove this sin and temptation from our lives, but we also want to remove it from everyone's life. Many men got their start in porn when they fished a magazine out of the trash. Erasing, breaking, cutting, shredding, and even burning physical stashes of pornography are nice visual reminders to ourselves and those we love that this is the value we put on pornography. We hug, kiss, and encourage our loved ones; we stomp, crush, and destroy pornography.

Removing Unhealthy Environments and Friendships

Your environment could be your greatest stumbling block outside of the physical presence of pornography. Either your environment is exposing you to pornography, or it's causing feelings that you are using porn to numb.

If you want to create a victorious environment, you need to look around and see if you're honestly walking out your daily life in a space that builds you up or tears you down.

The environments you inhabit daily are made up of both physical spaces and physical people. These elements of your environment should work together to inspire you to discover God's purpose for your life, as well as help you live out that purpose. If your environment is not allowing you to do both of these things, you need to alter it.

Some environments are just uninspiring to begin with. Perhaps you live in an apartment with little or no sunlight, or perhaps you are a night watchman, like one of the members of the X3LA group. While some men may thrive in dark and enclosed environments, others may not. The ensuing feeling of depression and isolation that can result from living or working in such a location may cause you to want to seek out a distraction. This is the right instinct, but if you are turning to pornography, it is the wrong action.

A better solution to this negative environment would be to change it. If you feel that your environment is causing you to use pornography, take the time *now* to physically change it. Change neighborhoods, change apartments, change bedrooms, change wall colorings, or change your housekeeping habits. If your work environment is unsavory, change jobs, change offices, change shifts. You may even be living with a woman outside of marriage. If you are, get married or move out.

Often a physical environment can be perfectly agreeable and positive but it can be filled with people who are not. It is essential to look at the people in your life and decide if they are healthy or unhealthy for you. It's obvious that any friend or relative who either remains committed to using pornography and/or doesn't respect your desire to stop using it is an unhealthy influence in your life. Also you may have friends or relatives who, while not actually involved in using pornography, cause many of your feelings that lead you to use pornography.

It is important to determine who in your life will encourage your sobriety and who won't, and then make decisions regarding changing, limiting, or eliminating your time with them. This is easier for some relationships than for others. It is relatively easy to redirect the conversations and activities of casual workplace acquaintances; it is much more difficult to do the same with a spouse or other family members.

Determine who in your life will encourage your sobriety and who won't.

The notion of changing, limiting, or eliminating unhealthy relationships can be complicated. You may not even know you're in an unhealthy relationship, or you may know but not understand how to change it. As a result of this confusion, you may continue to turn to pornography as an escape, a way to avoid the reality that things aren't healthy between you and someone else.

The specifics of repairing these relationships is outside the scope of this book, but we will say that if your close personal relationships are causing you damage by encouraging you to use pornography, you must take the time to change them. There is no other alternative.

If you are faced with a close relationship or marriage that is causing you pain, a good first step to healing is to openly confess to that person how you feel. If your confession is met favorably, then the two of you can begin to work together, or in conjunction with a therapist, counselor, or pastor, to seek healing. If your confession is not met favorably, still seek counsel from a therapist, counselor, or pastor. He will have ways to help you work through the challenges and issues you are personally facing. As we outlined in chapter 4, developing and restructuring your personal relationships is a key part of your recovery.

Psychologically Removing Triggers

While identifying the physical triggers that cause pornography use may be fairly clear and easy, actually avoiding them can be tough. For example, how do you remove that alluring Dolce & Gabbana billboard from outside your apartment window?

The opposite may be true of your psychological triggers. When you don't even know what's causing the emotions (such as feeling neglected, lonely, or confused) that lead to your using pornography, it's nearly impossible to deal with these triggers. When you understand the connection between certain emotions and your pornography use, you can begin to manage that side of your being.

Your brain is a very complex organ. There is a lot that goes into each individual brain and its development, and specific genetics, which are outside of your control, determine how your brain is structured. The way you were raised and treated as a child determines how you respond to the people, places, and events of this world. Every person's brain is specific to him or her, so generalizing psychological triggers can be dangerous.

We mentioned earlier that, after a child's first exposure to pornography, the chance that the child might become addicted to pornography as an adult increases by 5 percent each year until his brain is fully developed. We even suggested that early exposure to pornography could be considered a form of sexual abuse. Some men who struggle with porn were sexually abused as children or even as adults. Sexual abuse may cause a whole list of emotional states including fear, panic, irritability, and anger. If you were sexually abused at a young age, you may be turning to pornography as a way to mask feelings or as a way of expressing the confusion you feel about your sexuality.

Once again, this book is not equipped to detail the very deep psychological reasons that may trigger you to use pornography. If after using the tips and tools in this book, you are still not experiencing the freedom from pornography you are seeking, go to a professional counselor, therapist, or pastor to complete your goal for achieving healing. You *can* be free of pornography addiction; sometimes it's just a matter of how deep you are willing to dig.

Know, understand, embrace, and work toward your God-given purpose.

Now, despite the fact that targeting the cause of your psychological triggers may be a complicated undertaking, there are some techniques that you can use to help you manage them.

KNOWING YOUR PURPOSE

Many men get wrapped up in pornography because they have no clue what they should be doing with their lives. They do not know their God-given purpose and as a result lead their day-to-day existence responding to the circumstances they find themselves in instead of making choices about these circumstances. Honoring God is your number one aim in life. When you honor God, you know you are doing exactly what God wants you to do with your time on earth.

The best way psychologically to remove all sexual and nonsexual triggers from your life is to know, understand, embrace, and work toward your God-given purpose. We cannot stress this enough. If you are where God wants you to be, if you are waking each day to fulfill the demands he has placed on your life to fulfill, and if you have cleansed your life of all the obstacles that impede you from achieving your God-given purpose, you will experience the peace, fulfillment, and joy God has for your life, and you will have little or no desire to seek out and use pornography.

Not Responding to a Trigger

But remember, just because you have found and are working out God's purpose for your life, it doesn't mean something won't trigger your desire to use pornography. We live in a democratic society. Temptations abound and will even occasionally spring up in your face. In this reality, how can you immediately manage triggers psychologically?

Just because something has triggered your desire or you have recalled it from past experience, you don't have to continue entertaining the desire. It is possible to be exposed to a trigger and not let it cause sexual arousal, *even if you don't know what the trigger is or where it came from.*

There are numerous mental tricks men employ to manage their triggers psychologically. Some men will literally shake off the trigger, with their heads if need be, to remind them of where their focus should be. Other men will wear a rubber band around their wrist to snap when they catch themselves wanting to respond to their trigger. A favorite phrase in the X3LA Recovery Group is "parking your libido." When faced with a sexual trigger, you have the choice whether to keep your libido (that is, your sexual arousal) parked or to let it roll down the hill. Keep it parked and immediately go do something else!

Remaining Continually Confessional

Part of moving away from a physical or psychological trigger should include immediate confession to God, your accountability partner(s), your recovery small group, and/or your spouse. We discussed earlier the power of confession to lift the pressures many men feel in simply being and acting human. It's not a matter of *if* we are going to make a mistake in life; it's a matter of *when*. We are going to be exposed to sexual and nonsexual triggers; sometimes we may even mentally entertain those triggers when we shouldn't. While the triggers may be inevitable, actually having them lead us to using pornography is not.

Since the greatest tool for healing you have at your disposal is confession, you must remain continually confessional throughout each day. This means you start your day by confessing to God in prayer your weakness and powerlessness over pornography and asking him for his protection and power. When you are actually exposed to your sexual and nonsexual triggers, you can immediately confess to God what you saw and how it made you feel. He will help you. If you continue to feel triggered and led to pornography, call your accountability partner. The whole point of having a partner is to help prevent your use, not to make you feel better about yourself afterward.

This is a common mistake many men make when using confession as a tool in overcoming their addiction. While confession after using pornography might alleviate the self-hatred that perpetuates the cycle of the addiction, our goal here is to *avoid* using pornography in the first place. By talking with your accountability partner or spouse before you look at pornography, you can regain perspective over the triggers that may have caused you to want to use it. Maybe you are simply having a bad day and, by talking to your accountability partner, you can realize that you are not at the end of the world but at the dawn of a new day. Quite simply, your accountability partner may have some nice suggestions for activities that are immeasurably more productive than the hours you may spend in front of your computer using pornography.

The physiological reality is that once the brain's reward system is triggered, the neurochemicals that are released by it literally shut down or slow the functioning of the prefrontal cortex. This means that the more you give in to your sexual triggers, the more you override your brain's ability to reason and think your way out of being led to using pornography.

In many conversations we have had, counseling sessions we have conducted, or recovery message board posts we have read, we see a common sentiment: once you are triggered, it doesn't matter what someone says to you or what you know to be true about pornography; once triggered, you're simply going to use pornography no matter what. But this is not correct. The truth is that *the sooner you can confess your temptation and seek help, the easier it will be to pull yourself from this dangerous mental vortex*. It's up to you. Earlier in this chapter we discussed the importance of making small choices throughout your day. When tempted, immediately make the choice to confess. Don't let pornography's lies grip and destroy you.

Focus on the "Yes"

Sometimes the best decision you can make when triggered to use pornography, along with confessing to God and your accountability partner, is to simply find something positive to do. When Paul wrote in 1 Corinthians 6:18, "Flee from sexual immorality," he didn't intend for us just to run around aimlessly like a mouse without a hole. When he says to flee, he wants us to flee *toward* something. The most obvious place to which we should flee is to God and our God-given purpose; but sometimes, in the heat of the moment, it is perfectly acceptable to flee toward immediate pleasures that still honor God.

Maybe when you are triggered, you simply don't have the opportunity to refocus on something enjoyable. But this is telling. Are your job and personal relationships so unrewarding that, when you are triggered, they don't have enough draw to encourage you to refocus your attention on them? This is important. Once again, if your professional or personal environment is either triggering you to want to use pornography or isn't providing anything positive that holds your attention, it's imperative that you look at these environments and find ways to restructure them so you do find pleasure in them.

It is perfectly acceptable to flee toward immediate pleasures that still honor God.

We may not have a choice about our work or the people we have in our lives. If you find either or both unfulfilling, you need to focus on how to make them better. This should be your purpose and what is on your mind, rather than trying to escape through using pornography. Pornography use does nothing to move you toward a more fulfilling job or more pleasurable relationships; in fact it will only slow you down in the pursuit of either.

Whether you love your job or hate it, whether you're happily married or working on your marriage, whether you have good friends or are trying to find them, there are always—we repeat, always—better alternatives than looking at pornography. And the more pleasurable these alternatives are, the more enticing they will seem.

Sexual temptation will pass. It always does. When you are triggered, you may feel powerless over it at the moment, but give yourself five minutes of distraction and you may discover that the lies you have been told have little or no power. Seriously, try this the next time you are triggered. To change the focus of your brain, ignore the temptation by immediately standing up and going to do something other than what you were doing when you were triggered.

You may still be holding on to the lie that "I can't always just drop what I'm doing to go fly a kite!" but if you can find the time to drop all that you are doing to look at pornography for one, two, three, or even ten hours at a time, you can certainly take an hour or two to go eat ice cream, meet a friend for lunch, exercise, or build a model airplane.

"God-sanctioned activities" come in thousands of forms. Experiment with the ones that work for you. Take up new hobbies. Rediscover old passions. The writer of James 4:14 says, "What is your life? You are a mist that appears for a little while and then vanishes." Live *right now* for all of the things that matter to you, because the opportunity won't always be there.

A Note on Sex

Obviously, the most complete form of distraction from pornography for a married man would be sexual intercourse with his wife. There would be little else more satisfying when sexually triggered than finding sexual release within the confines of what God offers as a blessing. But with this outlet comes a few complications for the man who has used pornography as a sexual outlet in the past.

The first complication for many men who are addicted to pornography is that sex with their wife is no longer gratifying and therefore little help in alleviating the draw pornography has on them. Either the addicted man has so totally redefined what he finds sexually arousing that normal sex with his wife is now unsatisfying, or his addiction has become less about pornography itself and more about the ritualized practices of acquiring it (secrecy, location, using a certain computer, visiting particular websites, and so on).

In this case, the road to repairing your brain may be a longer haul; regardless, it can and will be done. As you work to starve this addiction, look at it as a significant success when you start to have sexual feelings toward your wife again. If that is the first goal you need to set for yourself, go ahead and set it.

On the other hand, if you still find sexual fulfillment with your wife, the greatest complication can be that she is not interested in sex, or not as interested as you are. There can be a number of reasons for this. Two of the most obvious are distrust and a lack of scriptural understanding.

Truly healthy and rewarding sex between a man and his wife involves a complicated network of trust and intimacy. When men have disrupted this network by going outside of their marriage for sexual fulfillment, it causes in the wife a high level of insecurity. In this context, a man asking his wife to help him through an addiction that has wounded her to her very core is like a soldier asking his enemy to help him out of a ditch right after he shot him.

Each marriage is unique, so offering solutions in this regard is difficult. Make sure you treat your spouse with the same respect you are expecting her to offer you. Just as you are working to recover from a wound, so is she. Sex in this context may be infrequent, but it may grow in frequency as your relationship heals and you and your spouse develop more trust in each other. This is a journey worth completing to its very end.

It may be wise to seek marriage counseling. There is never anything wrong in bringing in a respected third party to help you work through your relationship issues. This simple process can significantly accelerate the healing processes for both you and your wife and get you to a place where your addiction becomes less of an issue between the two of you. Additionally, during counseling, you may learn other reasons your wife is not as interested in sex as you are. Perhaps she was sexually abused at some point in her life; perhaps the process of sex is physically painful for her. Remember, sex is not the beginning and ending of life; it is simply part of it. Service to God—and this includes service to your wife—is your number one priority.

None of this is to deny the importance of sex in a marriage. As Paul wrote in 1 Corinthians 7:4–5:

> The wife's body does not belong to her alone but also to her husband. In the same way, the husband's body does not belong to him alone but also to his wife. Do not deprive each other except by mutual consent and for a time, so that you may devote yourselves to prayer. Then come together again so that Satan will not tempt you because of your lack of self-control.

Some wives may not totally understand this scriptural truth, that it is the wife's duty to help her husband sexually. But there is a flip side to this. Instead of shoving this Scripture in your wife's face to get what you want, you need to ask yourself honestly whether you've been living up to *your* scriptural obligations. This includes honoring God with your sexuality and keeping the marriage bed pure.

It is going to take some time for the intimacy within your marriage to be restored.

Sex with your wife is important, but again you must take into consideration the feelings, challenges, and emotions of your spouse as she too works through the issues your addiction has caused. Just as it's going to take time for your brain to recover from the abuse you have subjected it to over the years in looking at pornography, it is going to take some time for the intimacy within your marriage to be restored. Nothing worthwhile is ever easy, but as you repair your sexuality and your faith, the intimacy within your marriage will be strengthened as well.

- - - - - - - - - -

6

Go Time!

Accepting the Challenge

We cannot control the fate that will befall us, but we can
leave our imprint through the way we respond.

> —Rabbi Dayle A. Friedmann, "Sweet-
> ening the Bitterness of Suffering"

Here is where the rubber meets the road. We're going to
take all we've been discussing and actually apply it to *your*
life. There will be some repetition and some backtracking,
but since this challenge requires an inherent and absolute
dedication to your sobriety, you could stand to hear certain
principles again, until you get them into the very core of
your being.

The most important of these principles is that you are dead
to pornography. Yes, you are literally *dead* to it. What does
that mean? While you may still be exposed to pornography

or the triggers that cause your desire to use it, pornography is no longer an option for you. It is simply no longer an option. Just as a corpse is unresponsive to food, water, and air, you must believe that you are cold, numb, and dead to pornography.

Well, if you are dead to pornography, then what are you alive to? Christ. You are alive in Christ. When you first accepted Christ into your life—and we mean really accepted Christ into your life and believed that

If you are dead to

pornography, then

what are you alive to?

he is real and can heal and nurture you—you should have accepted the reality that you are now dead to this world. This world, and all of its lusts and temptations, is fleeting. This world will pass away, but life with Christ will not. It is in him that we find fullness and completion, nowhere else. We are dead to sin but alive in Christ (Col. 2:13–15).

Let's organize the basic aspects of your challenge, break them down personally for you, and provide you with concrete tools to ensure your sobriety.

Sobriety Sheets

There are two templates in the appendix of this book, two sheets that we want you to use: "Creating a Victorious Environment" and "Escape Plan." We will help you fill out these sheets and explain how to use them. You can fill out the pages provided in this book or make copies of them.

Sheet 1 will help you structure your life in a way that prevents triggers. Sheet 2 is your exit strategy for the times when you find yourself being drawn into pornography's grasp.

Please understand that these sheets are not independent of each other. We've designed them to "talk" to one another.

While you never want to allow yourself to become triggered, if it happens, there is a great deal you can learn about yourself and what is in your life that causes you to want to use pornography. As well, these sheets are not to be looked at as permanent "constitutions." They are tools that will change and grow along with you. In other words, as you heal, what was once a trigger for you may become meaningless. For example, perhaps you and your spouse are arguing less, or your lack of communication has disappeared altogether. Those issues with your spouse may no longer be a trigger, and the sheet will need to change to reflect that.

But don't be fooled. Losing one trigger doesn't mean another won't develop. Possibly the happiness and good cheer that replaced the friction in your marriage will trick you into thinking that pornography is now okay. It is not okay. Remember, pornography is *never* okay, and anything—we repeat, anything—that triggers you to use it must be avoided.

First Peter 5:8 warns us to "be self-controlled and alert. Your enemy the devil prowls around like a roaring lion looking for someone to devour." Your challenge with pornography will always be there. It may no longer have the same power over you, but you should never feel as if you are completely healed and over it. You have to be forever watchful, and maintaining the two Sobriety Sheets and keeping them handy will help you.

The goal of your Sobriety Sheets is to introduce "binary thinking" into your life (as we discussed in chapter 5). You're faced with thousands of choices every day. Some of these choices lead to life and others lead to death. If you can break down the choices you make daily and figure out which ones are healthy for you and which ones are not, you can be set free by continually making healthy choices.

There may be times when you will want to believe this lie: *No matter what I may be telling myself about using pornography, once I am triggered, there's nothing I can do.*

The truth is that there is always something you can do. It may not always be easy, and it may feel radical, but there is always something you can do.

- - - - - - - -
You have to be forever watchful.
- - - - - - - -

No one is going to be able to make the right choices for you. That is up to you. But if you can break down all the little decisions you make throughout the day, understand *on paper* which decisions you should be making, and then make the right decisions at the moment it matters, you will remain above the vortex of pornography's pull. This is "binary thinking." You are either making the right choices you have set yourself up to make or you are not. Period. So understand what the right choices are and then make them.

Sheet 1: Creating a Victorious Environment

Take time to examine Sheet 1. As the title says, you are going to start creating a victorious environment for yourself. There are two columns on the page: one that lists three sets of triggers and another that lists remedy actions for those triggers. Remedy actions represent the choices you need to make to help set you free from pornography. When you are triggered, you will choose either to use these remedy actions or not to use them.

There are five spaces for each trigger and their corresponding remedy actions, but you may want to list more. *The more triggers you can list and the more remedy actions you can decide on, the easier it will be for you to overcome this addiction.*

In the **Sexual Triggers** section, write down those immediate sexual triggers that cause you to want to use pornography. As a reminder, these triggers include the sights, sounds, textures, smells, or tastes of anything inherently sexual and can include men's magazines, seeing men or women in bathing suits, or R-rated movies. *You must list anything sexually related that triggers you to use pornography.*

Now fill in your remedy actions; these are the choices you should be making to avoid your triggers. If men's magazines are triggering you, your remedy action is *not to look at them*. If seeing men or women in bathing suits is a trigger, don't go where you might be exposed to men and women in bathing suits. If R-rated movies often trigger you, don't watch R-rated movies. This is about cleansing your life of pornography, not about whether you are in touch with pop culture.

In the **Nonsexual Environmental Triggers** section, write down any environmental triggers that make you want to use pornography. These could include the sights, sounds, textures, smells, or tastes of anything that is *not* inherently sexual in nature but still triggers you. It could be a certain computer, a certain person, the smell of a room, or even the color or colors that you have seen frequently on certain pornographic websites.

Nonsexual environmental triggers may seem difficult to pinpoint and list because they're not easily identifiable. But pay attention to the world around you. If you're feeling triggered and there is nothing inherently sexual within view, there is probably something within your environment causing you to think of, remember, or crave porn. Seem vague? Go ahead and list some items that *might* be an issue. Through time you may discover that they are not triggers at all and you can erase them from your list.

Once you have listed your nonsexual environmental triggers, list the corresponding remedy actions. If the sight of your computer is triggering you, get rid of it and get a new one. If being in a quiet house triggers you, play music. If the sight of certain colors triggers you, try to avoid them or at least recognize that they are triggers.

Nonsexual Emotional Triggers can also be difficult to identify. But once again, if you are feeling triggered, pay attention to your emotions at the moment. Are you experiencing any of the HALT feelings: hungry, angry, lonely, or tired? Are you sad or even happy at the time you feel triggered? If so, write these emotions down on your sheet.

Once you have listed your nonsexual emotional triggers, what remedy actions are you going to take to deal with these emotions? For example, when you are tired or overworked, you may need to take a day off once a week, start getting more sleep, or go on a few more vacations. You may think you don't have time to do these things, but if you have time to use pornography, you have time to get some sleep or go on a trip.

Look, we know that fixing emotional states is not the easiest thing to do. Sometimes these are the product of years of frustration or abuse, some of which may have come from your childhood. Finding the remedy action for certain emotions may become harder than you can figure out on your own. *But here's the truth: in these cases, porn is not the issue; your underlying emotional states are.* The sooner you accept this fact and deal with the causes, either on your own (with God's help) or with a therapist, counselor, or pastor, the sooner you will be set free from pornography's grip.

You may discover that your nonsexual environmental and your nonsexual emotional triggers have deep and profound connections. Maybe your boss angers you and your anger is a trigger that makes you want to use pornography. In this case, your boss is an environmental trigger and the anger you feel toward him is an emotional trigger. The remedy action for both of these triggers would be the same: work on your relationship with your boss or get a transfer.

Sheet 2: Escape Plan

Your Escape Plan is basically your evacuation strategy. If a hotel is burning down, you're more likely to survive if you have a detailed list of procedures for getting out of the building, know it by heart, and stick to it. Marines are instructed, trained, and drilled over and over again so that when they enter combat, they no longer think, they just do what they know they're supposed to do to survive. This is how you need to view your Escape Plan. It is your exit map; it is your way out of trouble. The better you structure it and know it, the greater your chance to avoid pornography when you are triggered to use it.

The Escape Plan has four elements. When you feel triggered, you will start at the top and do the things you have listed to get your mind back where it belongs. *Remember, the sooner you stop your sexual arousal, the easier it will be to avoid using pornography.* Your sexual arousal is like a boulder on top of a mountain. It's easy to stop that boulder from rolling down when it's at the top, but the farther it rolls down, the less chance you will have to stop it!

Your Escape Plan is your evacuation strategy.

The elements of your Escape Plan range in severity from the simple action of mentally and physically reminding yourself not to entertain your sexual arousal to the more drastic actions of doing something, anything that is positive, constructive, and God-sanctioned to avoid pornography use. It can be tough to remember, but your experience of being triggered *will* pass. If you are determined to overcome your addiction, there are plenty of things you can and should be doing to prevent use.

First on the Escape Plan are five spaces where you can list some good, strong mental and physical reminders that will help you keep your libido "parked" once you feel triggered to use pornography. Again, we can't stress enough the importance of stopping your sexual arousal *immediately*. These mental and physical reminders are any immediate thoughts or actions that you can employ at any point in time and at any place that will help you refocus your brain on the things God wants for your life.

Mental reminders could include simple things, such as saying to yourself, *I have so much more to live for* or *I will honor my wife whom I dearly love.* Many men memorize lines of Scripture to keep them focused on what matters most. Powerful verses include Proverbs 4:23–27 ("Guard your heart, for it is the wellspring of life . . .") and Psalm 23 ("The LORD is my Shepherd . . .").

Physical reminders could include simple actions like shaking your head or snapping a rubber band on your wrist when you begin to entertain inappropriate sexual thoughts.

Switch the focus of your brain to any God-honoring activity.

If these reminders aren't immediately helping you, and you are still feeling triggered, *it is your responsibility to immediately* **confess your feelings to God and your accountability partner.** The power of confession cannot be stressed too much. Simply admitting in prayer that you feel powerless and then asking God to help you in your time of need will relieve some of the pressures of working on your sobriety.

Beyond God there is no tool more powerful for your recovery than your accountability partner. When you are triggered, even if you feel you have your sexual arousal under control, call your accountability partner immediately. Share your feelings. Tell him where you are, what you are doing, and what you are going to do next. He may have suggestions, but most important he will understand your situation and validate your feelings.

Now comes the bulk of your Escape Plan, part 3. If you've been triggered, and you've both reminded yourself of your focus (mentally and physically) and spoken with God and your accountability partner, immediately switch the focus of your brain to *any* **God-honoring activity.** What activities do you love to do that you know God accepts and blesses?

The most obvious God-honoring focus is your life's purpose. If your purpose is still unclear, remember, every Christian's purpose is to love and honor God. If loving and honoring God is working at your current job so that you can get promoted, work that job with this in mind. If loving and honoring God is serving your family, spend time with your wife or play with your children. If loving and honoring God is serving your church, stop by; they'll likely have some fun community-building activities for you to do for the hour or two it takes to get refocused.

Beyond your purpose there are thousands of activities that God has blessed our world with other than pornography with which we can fill our time. By now you have most certainly remembered or discovered what some of these activities are. Now is your chance to write them down. Whatever you list, make sure they are activities that you love to do, activities that are infinitely more alluring and pleasurable than pornography. There is nothing wrong with going to a movie (as long as the movie doesn't have a rating or deal with a subject that is on your trigger list), going on a hike, riding a motorcycle, writing in a journal, working on a construction project—the list could go on for days.

But be very careful to choose activities you know God will approve. Replacing one addiction with another—like food, alcohol, or drugs—isn't going to provide you with freedom. If you are unclear as to whether a certain activity is "God-sanctioned," talk about it with your accountability partner, small group leader, or pastor. When you talk to your partner, you may discover some new things about yourself and your interests.

The last item on your Escape Plan sheet is **Revisit and Update Trigger Lists**. After you have made it through a triggering experience without using pornography, you have one more task to complete: identify the trigger that caused your sexual arousal. Once you have figured it out, check to see if it is on one of your trigger lists, then do the following:

1. If it isn't included in your trigger lists, figure out what type of trigger it was and add it with a corresponding remedy action.
2. If it is already listed, determine whether you were really following the remedy action you had planned. If not, now you know to be stricter in following that particular remedy action.
3. If the trigger is already listed and you followed the remedy action you had planned, reexamine your remedy action. For example, if seeing women in bathing suits or underwear is a trigger for you, and your remedy action for that trigger was to avoid beaches, yet you were triggered by walking past a Victoria's Secret store, maybe now you need to include as a remedy action steering clear of beaches *and* women's clothing stores, at least until you gain some healing.

Please do not undervalue the importance of this task! This is when you grow. We will never be perfect creatures, but we can experience heaven on earth through closeness with Christ. We draw closer and closer to him as we go through this process of continually improving ourselves through commitment to our sobriety and constantly searching to discover the hidden reasons we act out.

God is trying to show us something about ourselves to get us to a better place. The process is never easy, and the things we must face can sometimes be ugly. When we constantly work at creating a victorious environment for ourselves and stridently avoiding the sins that pull us farther away, God will expose to us the parts of our being—fear, trauma, self-doubt, anger—that are holding us back from being all that we can be. If it helps, keep a journal along with updating your Sobriety Sheets. Honest, confidential, and free-form expression of feelings and emotions in a written format is a safe and rewarding way to get to the core of your struggles and challenges.

The Sobriety Sheets are it. Our work is done; we've gone as far as we can. This is where your real work begins. You decide that either you are dead to pornography or you aren't. You either seek accountability or you don't. Fill out the Sobriety Sheets or choose not to. You either follow them or you don't. Update the sheets as you grow or decide not

Only you, with God's help, can make the decisions necessary to be sober.

to. It's that plain and simple. The path has been laid out. Only you, with God's help, can make the decisions necessary to be sober.

Many men, after filling out the sheets, have reduced them to pocket size and had them laminated, so they become portable reminders of the choices they need to make every second of every day. In doing this, they seldom needed to use them, as just the physical presence of the sheets is enough to keep them within the environment they know is healthy and to keep their sexual arousal under control if and when they happen to be triggered. Experiment with the best format for you, but make sure your sheets are close at hand.

What Will Going Sober Be Like?

Whether you realize it or not, every day or every second in which you have used pornography has been another day or second away from building healthy relationships and another day or second toward building unhealthy relationships. How long have you been using pornography? The longer it's been, the more revolutionary your change toward sobriety will be.

You've spent a lot of time developing a close personal bond with an imaginary friend while ignoring or eliminating bonds with real flesh-and-blood humans. The longer you used pornography, the further you distanced yourself from reality and the more difficult it will be for you to return to it. The good news? You *can* return. No matter how far away you got, you can always come back.

This experience is similar to that of a prison inmate. The longer an individual has been incarcerated, the longer he has spent time building up relationships with institutions and individuals whose realities are not based on civil society. Instead, relationships have been forged within an environment built on powerlessness, disrespect, and fear. This is the reality that the prisoner ends up knowing and understanding. It is where he feels most comfortable.

Many inmates, when they have been released back into society, don't know how to let go of what they knew in prison and, due to their inability to reintegrate into society, often repeat the same actions that put them in prison in the first place. According to the U.S. Department of Justice, two out of every three U.S. inmates who are released from prison will return to prison within three years.[3] If you have spent time in prison, we mean no disrespect in our comparison. If anything, we are empathizing with you by acknowledging the fact that once you have entered into a dysfunctional world, it's not easy to know what *functional* means. All compulsivity is a process of building a relationship with behavior and once that behavior is gone, there is a feeling of loss and a strong desire to return to it.

As many men can attest, going sober can be an other-worldly experience. If you are going sober, you really may feel as if you are losing a friend (and in essence you are—you're losing the worst friend you ever had, a friend who lies to you, cheats you, and steals from you). Ultimately it's like an abusive relationship where an individual systematically isolates you, twists the truth you once knew and understood, and keeps you under his control by telling you that the world you once knew doesn't understand you but that he does.

So what's it going to be like walking away from this "friend"? It's going to be scary, it's going to take a lot of courage, and most of all, it's going to take a lot of faith in God that all of the promises he offers you in Scripture really do exist, even if you can't quite see them (as Paul wrote in 2 Corinthians 5:7, "We live by faith, not by sight"). This fear of letting go of pornography will be just one of three potentially uncomfortable experiences you will have. The other two involve moving toward real relationships and physically healing from the damage done to your brain.

What's it going to be like walking away from this "friend"?

Overcoming Fear

In the end, walking away from using pornography is going to feel like letting go of a sharp, jagged rock in the middle of a violent ocean. That rock appears to be your only resting place, the only thing between you and death, the only thing that can sustain you, understand you, and meet your needs. It has told you that it will always be there for you, all the while ripping the flesh from your body with every wave that has pushed you against it.

But as you let go of that rock, you find not only that you can keep your head above water but that the ocean becomes less violent the farther away you drift from the rock. You discover a new resting place, one that is wide, soft, and gentle with plenty of shade, a cool breeze, and more food and fresh water than you can possibly use in a lifetime.

Real Relationships

Moving toward real relationships with individuals will come with its own set of challenges and expectations. Attending to and fixing broken relationships will take courage and honesty. But there is nothing to fear. If certain people aren't willing or capable of accepting you as you are, it's not your fault. Work to repair those relationships with honesty and, if needed, professional guidance from a counselor, therapist, or pastor. If repairing relationships in an open, honest context proves too difficult, maybe it's time to find new relationships.

Healing

In addition to repairing relationships, you may experience real physiological withdrawal symptoms including sleeplessness, lack of appetite, depression, fogginess of mind, and difficulty concentrating. Not only does prolonged pornography use strengthen neurological pathways in your brain to want and to seek pornography, but it also weakens the cerebral cortex, or the "thinking" part of the brain. Reversing this process will be challenging both in finding ways to resist your desire for pornography (for example, with your Sobriety Sheets) and in strengthening the thinking part of the brain (through mental exercises such as reading, writing, and discussion).

But remember, every second and every day that you abstain from pornography is another second and day of building new neurological pathways in the brain. It's another second and another day of getting stronger, healthier, and closer to God. It took you a while to get where you are and it might take you a while to get out of it. *But it can and will be done!*

It takes about ninety days from the last time you used pornography to start to feel normal again. But don't be fooled—you aren't completely healed in just ninety days. Your sobriety is now a major part of your life. Discipline, focus, and careful maintenance and review of your Sobriety Sheets *for years to come* are crucial. A big part of accomplishing all of this is remaining connected to a pornography recovery support group that will understand your challenges and help you become more relational.

Many men and women who have gone sober from substances of abuse commemorate a new "birthday." This birthday is the day they stopped using drugs, alcohol, or pornography. Commemorate that day. The more time since the day that you have been sober will be more incentive to stay clean. After all, who wants to return to the beginning of a battle after he has fought his way out of it?

Don't be too hard on yourself. Jesus isn't.

Despite all of these conditions that you may be feeling as you go sober, please remember that no matter how you are feeling, as long as you are no longer using pornography, *you are right where you need to be.*

Don't be too hard on yourself. Jesus isn't.

X3LA Recovery Group

The time the X3LA Recovery Group has spent together has been remarkable. As a team of more than fifty men, they have traveled through the major steps of recovery—acceptance to accountability, education to planning, and commitment to healing. While all of these steps have been made easier for individual members by working as a team, no step has required more continual support than the Sobriety Sheets.

Directly after the first time the Sobriety Sheets were presented, a number of the men contacted Steven to suggest that maybe their current meeting schedule of every other week should be changed to once a week (as of the printing of this book, some men meet with Steven or the other leaders of the X3LA group as many as two times a week). These members were starting to realize that becoming and remaining sober was going to require a lot of commitment, a lot of dedication, a lot of strength, and a lot of support from like-minded men. In these meetings, members have had the opportunity to voice their struggles, be heard, and make changes.

For instance, Chris was able to share his realization that he was afraid to let go of pornography. He was afraid, because letting go meant that he would never get it back. Not only was he afraid to let go, he was feeling foggy in the brain and had difficulty concentrating. With the help of the X3LA support group, Chris was able to see that his condition was both psychological and physiological. He was afraid to let go of pornography because it would mean he would have to face his fears, certain relationships, and the state of his life in general; he was feeling foggy and had a difficult time concentrating because the rewired circuitry of his brain was screaming for the stimulation (pornography) of which it had been deprived.

These realizations helped Chris put his experiences and feelings into context and helped him through another week. Chris was even given the opportunity to share that as a computer-savvy professional, he had easily figured out ways to bypass both his computer's filtering and accountability software. While this confession wasn't enough to prevent him from doing it (unfortunately), the painful experience of divulging that he had breached his remedy actions forced him to reexamine his triggers. Looking at them, he's realizing that his parents' divorce, his father's suicide, and his stepfather's belittling him created an acute identity crisis, and when he feels the emotion of not knowing who he is, he runs to pornography as an escape. *Now that's growth!*

Trent, another member, was able to share what some may see as a small accomplishment but what was a huge milestone for him. Earlier in the week he had purchased a new novel. As he read it, he could see that there were going to be depictions of sex and, instead of continuing on, knowing full well that books like these were on his trigger list, he put the book immediately in the recycling bin.

Yes, his group was proud of him, but Trent had more to add and share. He admitted that in the process of eliminating all sexual triggers from his life, he was starting to feel a little lost, a little confused. He didn't quite know what God wanted from him or where he was going with his life. While the group did help him initially to begin to sort out where and what he should be doing, the most important thing they were able to do was validate his feelings and assure him that in openly facing the world without pornography, he was right where he was supposed to be.

Devin was able to share successes that the rest of the world may not be able to appreciate or understand, but successes everyone in the group was able to learn from. As he's gone sober, these successes have included an ability to experience wet dreams again, become sexually aroused without the use of pornography, and even make love to his wife the way God had intended it to be: with pride, dignity, and honor. This was not only encouraging for Devin but for the group as well, as many of the members were experiencing some of the

God never meant for us to work alone.

same sexual dysfunction he once experienced. Seeing that there was an end to that trauma gave them hope.

We could go on and on with testimonies that underscore the power and purpose of accountability groups (for instance, Aaron was able finally to accept his need to become account-able to himself and the men in his group once he realized that every evening he showed up for group, he would be asked whether or not he had used pornography in the past week; Carlos, only twenty-four, could see and understand that his sexual drive was normal but that he needed to find other ways to "blow off steam"). Meeting in groups of like-minded people is going to get you through this process of healing. God never meant for us to work alone; it is when we are isolated that the devil can plant his most damaging seeds.

If you don't belong to a recovery group, please find one. If your church doesn't have one, create one. If your church isn't interested in supporting you in creating one, join a group at a church that does. Whatever you do, seek support through consistent relationship-building meetings. Your sobriety depends on it.

If you need curriculum for your group, consider using this book, chapter by chapter, meeting by meeting. We also have a DVD and a workbook as well as a leader's guide available. Email **info@XXXchurch.com** for those resources.

◆■◆

To facilitate each meeting, and help ensure that each group member gets a chance to talk, go around the room and have everyone respond to the statements listed below:

Meeting Statements

1. State your first name and how long you have been sober.
2. State the closest experience you have had to using the object of your addiction (porn, masturbation, strip clubs, etc.) since the last meeting, what your trigger was, and what you did about it.
3. If you were triggered, and this trigger was new, please add it to your Sobriety Sheets. If it wasn't new, were you honestly obeying your "remedy action" for this trigger? If not, how can you change your remedy action to meet the needs for avoiding this trigger in the future?
4. State one lie you have told someone in the past week or a secret you are keeping from someone else or the group.
5. State three positive affirmations about yourself. For example, "I am a valuable and loved member of my community."
6. In one or two words, state how you are feeling emotionally right now.

Members responding to these statements will be forced to face their challenges head-on and discover more about themselves than they possibly could have known on their own. As a result, their Sobriety Sheets will be easier to maintain and follow.

7

Grab Your Shovel

Embracing Your Faith

To trust in God calls for attention to what God is doing, to making oneself sensitive to what God requires, to aligning one's will with God's aims and call. It requires a shift from an attitude of control and manipulation to one of openness and receptivity. Discernment and discrimination become more important than trying to shape events to meet the projected goals. Of course, the God who speaks to us in the life processes of our bodies and souls addresses us also through other people, through tradition, and especially through those saints and spiritual giants who have lived from and for God with peculiar fullness. We can test our discernment against theirs and in community with others who seek to understand God's call today.

John Cobb, *Pastoral Care and Counseling*

We have provided you with the healing tools you need; the rest is up to you.

You have to want it. You have to want it more than anything you have ever wanted in your whole life, and then you have to follow through with your Sobriety Sheets and recovery group attendance.

While we emphasize the importance of your individual determination, we stress equally the reality that as a Christian, you are not alone. Yes, you do have your accountability partner and your recovery group, but you also have on your side the single most powerful Helper in the universe. We are, of course, referring to God.

You have on your side the single most powerful Helper in the universe.

If God is the single most powerful Helper in the universe, why are we waiting until now to discuss your relationship with him? Two reasons: first, we needed to help you understand the physiological realities of this addiction, that porn has changed your brain, and that, before you can feel normal again (or even capable of thinking straight), you have to have some initial healing. Second, we needed to explain and express the reality that an addiction to pornography is not about pornography itself but about masking the pains, hurts, frustrations, and confusions inherent in your life.

Now that we have done that, we are ready to focus on the ultimate answer to your addiction—the power and love of God, the One who can meet all your needs and bring you to victory.

If you have honestly stuck to your Sobriety Sheets, avoiding pornography *at all costs* while simultaneously updating your sheets to really get to the core of what is causing you to want to use pornography, you are undoubtedly unearthing challenging aspects of your being. Perhaps you were abused as a child, perhaps you lost your wife because of your addiction, perhaps you suffered a traumatic experience in the military, or perhaps you feel as if you have failed in some aspect of your life. Realizing these things about yourself is hard enough, but now what are you going to do about them and the feelings they have engendered?

Yes, there is therapy, and we seriously support and recommend pursuing it. There are many options, including one-on-one counseling available at your church or personal counseling at local counseling centers. Some even provide services on a sliding scale or for free. Speak with someone at your church to discover what options may be available.

But along with this kind of therapy, the greatest therapy you can receive, the kind that goes deep into your soul and searches out all of those hurting places to bring light, love, and healing, is the kind of therapy God offers for free, 24-7, around the clock.

How do we access this supernatural healing? There are many paths, some of which you may have tried. If you have never tried accessing God's healing power, here are some of the most powerful "faith tools" available to you. If you feel as if you have tried accessing God's power in doing some of these things but have come up short, this summary may prove helpful in reevaluating the way you're approaching your faith.

Stepping into the Void

We have already pointed out the gap that lies between realizing the deep things in our being that cause us to use pornography and achieving the peace and freedom we desire. We hurt. We hurt from things that have happened to us or from things we have or haven't done. That's where we are. Presumably, we want to be in a place where we no longer hurt, where we feel no pain, and where we achieve a sense of peace, contentment, and focus.

That place of peace, contentment, and focus is union with God. Paul wrote in 1 Corinthians 14:33, "God is not a God of disorder but of peace." In Psalm 85:8 the writer said, "I will listen to what God the LORD will say; he promises peace to his people, his saints." And God wants us to live with him. "For God so loved the world that he gave his one and only Son, that whoever believes in him shall not perish but have eternal life" (John 3:16). In other words, God doesn't just want us to be okay—he wants us to be exalted and ecstatic. He doesn't just want us to be sober, although that's a good starting point—he wants us to be fulfilled and alive.

So how do we go from where we are—realizing the hurts, struggles, and frustrations that have led us to using pornography—to where we need to be, in concert and union with God? There are a number of action steps, but they all lead up to one central principle: faith.

Every day, we have faith in a number of things. We have faith when we cross the street that the cars approaching the crosswalk will stop when the light is red. We have faith when we get on a plane that it will land at its intended destination. We have faith when we eat food at a restaurant that it won't make us sick.

> *So how do we go from where we are to where we need to be?*

And there are larger areas of faith. We have faith that we will overcome illnesses. We have faith that we will go to heaven when we die. Ultimately we have faith that God really does exist.

Essentially, when we turn to pornography as an escape from our realities, we are lacking faith that God can and will heal those portions of our soul that are hurting; we are lacking faith that by giving those hurts, pains, and frustrations to him, instead of masking them with pornography, he can and will find ways for us to manage them.

But how do we start letting go? How do we stop trying to manage what we can't manage, step into the void of faith, and trust that God will help us through what we can't get through on our own? There are eight basic practices that God lays out for us in Scripture, eight basic action steps that can tenderize our hearts, relax our souls, deepen our perspective, and, in the end, alleviate the worries that led us to porn in the first place. These action steps are spending time in Scripture, daily prayer, weekly church attendance, weekly Bible study or small group attendance, service to God, tithing, fasting, and honestly respecting the Sabbath. If you can consistently and honestly take these eight action steps, *you will be making room for God's healing touch.*

Spending Time in Scripture

When many Christian men realize they have a problem, their first inclination is to pray. They get on their knees and they ask God to take this thing away from them. This is a wonderful instinct, but those prayers usually go unanswered.

Why? Certainly not because God isn't listening—he is. But God isn't going to supernaturally cure someone of something unless he can help the person get to the cause of the affliction. God isn't interested in masking your pains; after all, isn't that what the false god of pornography did for you? Our God is a real God, and when you ask him for healing, he's going to help you understand what he is healing you from and why. God doesn't want us to just *look* good; he wants us to *be* good, from the inside out.

While you may look to God for help and direction through prayer, it's easy to forget that God has already given you help and direction through the Bible as well. The Bible offers counsel, nurture, hope, and peace. Once you understand this, you can use Scripture to gain the power and strength necessary to overcome temptation.

The most important aspect of using Scripture to gain strength is to understand that it is alive. The words written in the Bible come from inspired reflection. The writer of Hebrews 4:12 said, "For the word of God is living and active. Sharper than any double-edged sword, it penetrates even to dividing soul and spirit, joints and marrow; it judges the thoughts and attitudes of the heart."

Since the words in the Bible are alive, reading them daily is a great reminder of the Lord's goodness and his deep desire to protect you from evil and to strengthen you in your weakness. For example, James 4:7 says that when you submit yourself to God and resist the devil, *the devil will flee from you.* Paul wrote in 1 Corinthians 10:13, "No temptation has seized you except what is common to man. And God is faithful; he will not let you be tempted beyond what you can bear. But when you are tempted, he will also provide a way out so that you can stand up under it."

One of the most important things to remember is that God sent a Helper in the Holy Spirit to reside in you and give you strength and counsel (John 14:16–17). The Holy Spirit led the writer of 1 John 4:4 to declare, "The one who is in you is greater than the one who is in the world."

Knowledge of the Holy Spirit and his power gives life to other portions of Scripture, including the two most significant chapters for individuals struggling with addictions, especially pornography. In Romans 7–8 Paul discusses the power sin can gain over us simply because we want to live by the laws God created for us. The pressure we feel in trying to be "perfect" causes us to become slaves to sin. Paul says in Romans 7:15, "I do not understand what I do. For what I want to do I do not do, but what I hate I do." In Romans 7:18–19 he says, "For I have the desire to do what is good, but I cannot carry it out. For what I do is not the good I want to do; no, the evil I do not want to do—this I keep on doing."

We are under a new law, that of the Holy Spirit.

These feelings Paul expresses are the very feelings many Christian men experience when they are trying desperately to free themselves from pornography use. When they fail, they hate themselves all that much more because they want to do right by God but feel helpless. What these men are missing, says Paul, is the understanding that it is *impossible* for us to live by God's laws through our own effort. In fact, he says, it is our own effort that *creates* sin inside of us because of our inability to keep the law on our own.

Paul stresses that it is only through Christ Jesus and the Holy Spirit God so graciously gave us that we can overcome sin. "The law of the Spirit of life sets us free from the law of sin and death" (Rom. 8:2). As followers of Christ, we are under a new law, that of the Holy Spirit.

> For what the law was powerless to do in that it was weakened by the sinful nature, God did by sending his own Son in the likeness of sinful man to be a sin offering. And so he condemned sin in sinful man, in order that the righteous requirements of the law might be fully met in us, who do not live according to the sinful nature but according to the Spirit. Those who live according to the sinful nature have their minds set on what that nature desires; *but those who live in accordance with the Spirit have their minds set on what the Spirit desires. The mind of sinful man is death, but the mind controlled by the Spirit is life and peace.*
>
> Romans 8:3–6, emphasis added

Read the Bible daily with these concepts in mind: the Word is alive, and when you accepted Christ into your life, you accepted the Holy Spirit, from whom you can gain strength and on whom you can focus your attention instead of on pornography. Remember, *you are dead to pornography, but alive in Christ*. Accept now that you are dead to this world and all of its temptations. Eternity with God is your real reward.

Commit yourself to spending just a few minutes per day reading your Bible. Don't kill yourself trying to read it from cover to cover, either. Start with a favorite Gospel, such as

Matthew or John. Read encouraging Epistles, like Romans or Galatians. Scour Psalms and Proverbs. You can set up your own Bible reading plan online at **www.youversion.com** and click on New Reading Plans.

Here's a good Scripture you can write on a note card or jot down in your journal to help you remain committed to your daily Bible reading. It's Psalm 119:9–12: "How can a young man keep his way pure? By living according to your word. I seek you with all my heart; do not let me stray from your commands. I have hidden your word in my heart that I might not sin against you. Praise be to you, O LORD; teach me your decrees."

Daily Prayer

As you understand the true nature of Scripture, your prayers will have much deeper meaning to both you and God. In following God's scriptural expectations for you, you will have the confidence and certainty of heart to ask God openly for the blessings he promises his followers. Conversely, when you have failed to meet God's expectations as revealed through Scripture (and you will!), you can boldly come before God in prayer to accept the forgiveness he so generously provides.

So how does all of this play out in practice? Many men feel as if they have lost so much ground with God that they have no right to pray to him. Sometimes they feel they don't know how to pray "correctly" or "fervently enough," and it inhibits their connection with God.

Please don't put so much pressure on yourself! God wants to meet you right where you are. He wants to talk with you, he wants to show you his love, and he wants to listen to you. Like the lover in Song of Songs 2:14, God wants to "hear your voice; for your voice is sweet, and your face is lovely." Isaiah 30:18–19 reads: "Yet the LORD longs to be gracious to you; he rises to show you compassion. For the LORD is a God of justice. Blessed are all who wait for him! O people of Zion, who live in Jerusalem, you will weep no more. How gracious he will be when you cry for help! As soon as he hears, he will answer you."

If you don't know how to approach God in prayer, simply come to him as your loving and caring Father and thank him for all he has done and ask him for what you need. You can pray something like this: "Lord, thank you

God wants to meet you

right where you are.

for being my Father. Thank you for being a good God who cares for me and loves me. Thank you for sending your Son Jesus Christ to die on the cross so that I could be made free. Thank you, Jesus, for dying for my sins. Lord, I give you everything I am—my talents and my sins. I freely submit to you and ask that you give me strength today to make the most of what you have given me and resist and overcome temptation. In Jesus's name I pray, Amen."

Your goal in prayer is not to pray perfectly or correctly (because there's no right way), it is just to acknowledge that God is your Father and that you are after his will. Open yourself to his leading by the Holy Spirit and remind yourself that God is in control of your life, not you. And most of all, ask God for his direction and deliverance—he wants so much more for you than you want for yourself. "Let us then approach the throne of grace with confidence, so that we may receive mercy and find grace to help us in our time of need" (Heb. 4:16).

Be sure to pray daily, and you may want to pray many times a day to keep you aware of the fact that God is near and is ready to help you.

Weekly Church Attendance

No form of submission to God could be simpler or clearer than just showing up at church on Sunday. Some say there's no scriptural basis for going to church, citing Galatians 2:16, which points out: "A man is not justified by observing the law, but by faith in Jesus Christ." Yes, you are and always will be saved whether you go to church or not, as long as you still "confess with your mouth, 'Jesus is Lord,' and believe in your heart that God raised him from the dead" (Rom. 10:9). But is that all you want for your life? God certainly has more in store for you than just being saved. He wants you to experience heaven on earth (see Matt. 6:10).

The best way to grow into the person God would like you to be, which includes your sobriety, is to get plugged into a local church and regularly attend services. Paul wrote in 1 Timothy 3:15 that the church is the pillar and foundation of the truth. It is in church that you will receive knowledge and direction. It is in church that you will hear the "gentle whisper" of God (1 Kings 19:12). Christ said in Matthew 18:20, "Where two or three come together in my name, there am I with them."

Since God is present in church gatherings, when you attend services you are drawing near to him, and as you draw near to him, he will draw near to you (James 4:8). And if you want more of God, more of his presence and more of his protection, don't just show up—expand your praise. Sit in the front. Participate in the worship time *whether it feels comfortable or not*. This is about submitting to the will of the great Healer. God sees your dedication to his purpose and he will bless and protect your life.

Remember, a big part of overcoming your addiction is becoming more relational and involving yourself with real flesh-and-blood humans. There is no better or safer place to experience these relations than in church.

Weekly Bible Study or Small Group

As you grow in your connection to your church, branch out and join a Bible study or small group. You'll meet like-minded people and be given the chance to wrestle with confusing or challenging aspects of your faith and get to the heart of issues directly affecting you.

While we stress the importance of creating or joining a pornography support group, there are other Bible studies or small groups that will benefit you as well because they will provide opportunities for you to grow in the Word and expand your faith.

When you are recovering from a pornography addiction, sometimes it's good to find a Bible study or small group that meets in the middle of the week. Often the wonderful reminders God gives you of your value and importance during Sunday services wear off as the week progresses, and you can find yourself increasingly vulnerable to the enemy's attacks. Joining a strong and supportive gathering of like-minded believers on a Wednesday can refocus your brain and help you see the importance and significance of your sobriety before it's too late. Also the chances of being sexually triggered decrease dramatically when you're sitting around your friend's living room or in a church basement!

Submit our talents and abilities to him in service.

Service to God

Much of pornography addiction is caused by putting too much focus and attention on ourselves. We stress and worry about what we're supposed to be getting out of life, and we try to control our lives and get frustrated, instead of accepting that ultimately we are not in control. Frustration may lead us to turn to things that make us feel good in the moment, like pornography.

Since God is in control of everything, we need to learn to submit our talents and abilities to him in service. In doing so, we relax the pressure we create for ourselves to be perfect, and we lessen the power pornography has over our lives. Plus, when we serve, we achieve more of our own human potential (including being pornography-free) than we would have if we had not thought about the needs of others.

In essence, when we "weaken" ourselves in God's name by being submissive to him, we allow him to enter our lives and make the most of all that we have to offer. Jesus said in Matthew 20:26–28, "Whoever wants to become great among you must be your servant, and whoever wants to be first must be your slave—just as the Son of Man did not come to be served, but to serve, and to give his life as a ransom for many." Paul emphasized this message in Colossians 3:23–24 by saying, "Whatever you do, work at it with all your heart, as working for the Lord, not for men, since you know that you will receive an inheritance from the Lord as a reward. It is the Lord Christ you are serving."

As you may know, there are many service opportunities available to you at your church. These range from ushering to working in the nursery, working with youth, audio/visual teams, neighborhood cleanup, feeding the poor, and tons more, and those are just examples within churches. Beyond your home church there are literally hundreds of ministries, including homeless shelters, soup kitchens, pregnancy resource centers, and tutoring centers. There is no excuse for not being able to find a place to get plugged in. And if there doesn't appear to be a place, *create one*!

In addition to honoring God with your talents, service gives you an opportunity to build new real-life friends and relationships that will help your body and mind recover from the effects of pornography use. Not only that, but it will also give you a broader perspective on your value and worth.

Tithing

Ah . . . the wallet. It's never an easy topic to discuss, in or outside of church.

We live in a country largely geared toward financial success. Most Americans' goals are wrapped up in the American dream of career advancement, bigger houses, nicer cars, and greater material provision. Look around. *Money* is the goal of our society, not God.

Disagree? Think of the many stresses that govern our lives, the stresses that lead many men to porn. These stresses include those caused by making mortgage payments; working too many jobs; not working enough jobs; needing to pay cable bills, electric bills, phone bills, gas bills. Advertisements bombard us daily, letting us know that there is more to be had and implying that we're missing out if we don't have it.

The people selling these products aren't trying to bless us with something we need; they just want our money. The same is true, of course, with the pornographers. They aren't making pornography because they like sex; they make it because they know you're willing to pay them for it.

The wallet. It's never an easy topic to discuss.

More than any other topic discussed during his ministry on earth, Jesus discussed money. He knew it had the greatest power to corrupt our hearts and turn us away from loving and honoring God. "No one can serve two masters," Jesus said in Matthew 6:24. "Either he will hate the one and love the other, or he will be devoted to the one and despise the other. You cannot serve both God and Money."

This does not mean that there is anything wrong with pursuing, acquiring, or using money. Paul wrote in 1 Timothy 6:10, "For the *love of money* is a root of all kinds of evil. Some people, eager for money, have wandered from the faith and pierced themselves with many griefs" (emphasis added). When we *love* money and make it the center of our lives so that it influences how we live, we will eventually become frustrated or unfulfilled, and both of these emotions can lead directly to the "grief" of pornography use. Paul wrote in 1 Timothy 6:9, "People who want to get rich fall into temptation and a trap and into many foolish and harmful desires that plunge men into ruin and destruction."

If God provides money and material blessings, how do you keep your "love of money" in check, protecting yourself from "ruin and destruction"? It's really very simple, and God is pretty clear on this principle in verse after verse in the Bible. Even before God instructs us in Leviticus 27:30 that "a tithe of everything from the land, whether grain from the soil or fruit from the trees, belongs to the LORD; it is holy to the LORD," Abraham gave the high priest Melchizedek "a tenth of everything" (Gen. 14:20).

For those who are unaware, a tithe is 10 percent of your income. You are instructed by God to *return to him* 10 percent of the increase he has blessed you with. This is 10 percent of your paycheck, 10 percent of your investment earnings, even 10 percent of that cash your grandparents gave you when you turned eighteen!

Begin tithing. You'll see God show up.

Some Christian men balk at bringing their tithe to church for fear that the money will be mismanaged or misspent. But tithing isn't about "proper use of funds." Just as the time you offer God in service is more about your devotion than it is about the service itself, bringing your 10 percent to the Lord is about submission. If you are worrying about your tithe being used effectively, you are trying to control what you can't control. Your desire to control all the aspects of your life led you into addiction. Letting go and trusting God will get you out of it.

When you give up control of your finances to God, he gives you the things money can't buy, like joy, happiness, pleasure, and excitement. In trusting God with your money, he can orchestrate so much more for you than you can orchestrate for yourself. You want to break the chokehold of pornography addiction? Prayerfully and submissively begin tithing. You'll see God show up. Guaranteed.

God says in Malachi 3:10, "Bring the whole tithe into the storehouse, that there may be food in my house." But God doesn't stop there. *He then offers the only opportunity in the Bible for us to test his goodness.* "Test me in this," he says, "and see if I will not throw open the floodgates of heaven and pour out so much blessing that you will not have room enough for it."

Fasting

At the root of both service to God and tithing is the principle of weakening yourself in the name of the Lord so that you'll be open to hearing his voice, being enlarged by him, and being cured of things you can't cure on your own. This process of weakening could also be called "fasting."

Fasting is generally defined as abstaining from food for a specified period of time, but there is no exact prescription for fasting in the Bible. When we wish to refocus our mind and spirit on God to invite him more fully into our life by voluntarily weakening ourselves through fasting, we open up the opportunity for God's strength to enter us.

Don't enter into fasting lightly. Your goal in fasting is not to punish yourself or to boast of your piety. In Matthew 6:16 Jesus said, "When you fast, do not look somber as the hypocrites do, for they disfigure their faces to show men they are fasting." The goal is to refocus your attention on the one true Source of your fulfillment and to break the bonds of false gods, such as pornography. "When you fast," continued Jesus, "put oil on your head and wash your face, so that it will not be obvious to men that you are fasting, but only to your Father, who is unseen; and your Father, who sees what is done in secret, will reward you" (vv. 17–18).

Practically speaking, fasting from food can take on many different forms. If fasting appears to be a faith tool that will help you begin to refocus your life and soul on God instead of on your challenges with overcoming an addiction to pornography, try picking a day of the week when you would especially benefit from your faith being increased, perhaps a day of the week when you feel most tempted to use pornography or a day of the week when you feel you face the greatest number of triggers. Perhaps you wish only to fast one day per month. Whatever day you choose, make sure that your fasting has as its goal refocusing your life on God, not ritualistically observing some "law."

Usually fasting involves avoiding food, not water (please don't stop drinking water; it is essential for life). Some people may fast only from certain items, such as meat or animal products. Whatever you choose, please be mindful of your health and avoid going to extremes and causing personal damage or harm. Remember, our goal with fasting is to strengthen our faith and even strengthen our bodies. We are not after self-punishment or self-abuse. Jesus forgave our sins on the cross. Our job as humans is to continue to try to improve ourselves by drawing closer to him.

Fasting isn't solely about food.

As we mentioned, fasting isn't solely about food. Just as with time and money, there are other worldly pleasures from which we can abstain for days, weeks, or even permanently so that we may refocus our attention where it belongs. As a general rule of thumb, if you feel as if you are putting something before God, even if it isn't "technically" considered a sin yet it is interfering with your hearing God's voice, as an action of deference to God, you can fast from it.

For instance, many men today may not realize how much entertainment has interfered with and muted God's voice in their lives. Not only do hours of watching TV, movies, and sports consume time that could be devoted to building and pursuing our God-given purpose, but it also bombards our minds, and therefore our spirituality, with a secular perspective of how the world works. No wonder we get confused! There is nothing wrong with entertainment, but when our entertainment begins to take precedence over our time with God, it's time to go on a media fast.

For more in-depth discussion on different kinds of fasting, see Craig's book *Starving Jesus*, or Lynne Baab, *Fasting: Spiritual Freedom beyond Our Appetites*.

Honestly Respecting the Sabbath

In Exodus 20:8–11 God says,

> Remember the Sabbath day by keeping it holy. Six days you shall labor and do all your work, but the seventh day is a Sabbath to the LORD your God. On it you shall not do any work, neither you, nor your son or daughter, nor your manservant or maidservant, nor your animals, nor the alien within your gates. For in six days the LORD made the heavens and the earth, the sea, and all that is in them, but he rested on the seventh day. Therefore the LORD blessed the Sabbath day and made it holy.

Many of us consistently fail to follow this commandment because we are guilty of breaking the first commandment, which is "You shall have no other gods before me" (v. 3).

In the United States we may be bowing down to the god of money. Once again, there is nothing wrong with achieving success and acquiring money, but when we lose perspective of who blesses us with both (God), we set ourselves up for attack by the enemy through stress, worry, frustration, and greed.

Observing the Sabbath is a simple way of letting God know that he is supreme in our life and in charge. When on Sunday we offer up to him our time by attending church, spending time with family and friends, and resting, he can and will make time for us to do the other things we need to do in life, including work. Obviously there is wisdom in God's commandments and we shouldn't question them; instead we should consider their power to improve our lives.

At the end of Isaiah 58, the same chapter that discusses "true fasting," God speaks in verses 13 and 14 about the importance of respecting the Sabbath and setting it aside as a holy day:

> If you keep your feet from breaking the Sabbath and from doing as you please on my holy day, if you call the Sabbath a delight and the LORD's holy day honorable, and if you honor it by not going your own way and not doing as you please or speaking idle words, then you will find your joy in the LORD, and I will cause you to ride on the heights of the land and to feast on the inheritance of your father Jacob.

The Blessing of Faith

Your faith is the most powerful tool you have available to overcome your addiction. When you accepted Christ as your Lord and Savior, you did not accept some impossible goal of perfection. Instead, you invited the Holy Spirit into your very being as your Counselor, sent by God in Jesus's name, to "teach you all things" and "remind you of everything [Jesus] has said to you" (John 14:26).

Your faith is the most powerful tool you have available to overcome your addiction.

As Paul said in Philippians 4:13, "I can do everything through him who gives me strength." Our faith in Christ isn't just an obscure idea that directs our actions. Our faith provides the way for the very real Spirit of God to live inside of us, giving us the power to surmount the seemingly insurmountable. Overcoming an addiction to pornography is a process of finding a way when there appears to be no way. By enlarging the Holy Spirit's involvement in our life through closeness with God in the ways we have outlined above, we accept the truth of Isaiah 54:17 that "no weapon forged against you will prevail."

We discussed "binary thinking" in regard to our Sobriety Sheets, and you can apply "binary thinking" to your faith. Once you receive Christ as your Savior, which is a binary decision, and the Holy Spirit is in you, it is up to you to choose how much access to your soul you allow him. Through binary decisions you make each day, you can allow him more access and thus reset your focus on God. In resetting your focus on God, you can experience more of his presence in your life, more of his direct guidance, and, most significantly, more of his *divine intervention*. As the writer of Hebrews 11:6 pointed out, "without faith it is impossible to please God, because anyone who comes to him must believe that he exists and that *he rewards those who earnestly seek him*" (emphasis added).

You may be thinking, *But faith is such a vague notion!* It isn't, really. Just as you have to break down your Sobriety Sheets into the smallest remedy actions possible and then choose to take those remedy actions when it matters most, you can also break your faith down into the smallest remedy actions. Either you're reading the Word daily or you aren't; either you're praying daily or you aren't; either you're attending church or you aren't; either you're attending a weekly Bible study or small group or you aren't; either you're serving God weekly or you aren't; either you're tithing or you aren't; either you're fasting or you aren't; either you're observing the Sabbath or you aren't.

Just as your addiction is not about pornography, your challenge is not just about beating the devil; it's about letting God show you what's holding you back from your potential. Let go of the past, let go of the future, and let God dictate the direction of your life. Ephesians 4:22–24 says, "You were taught, with regard to your former way of life, to put off your old self, which is being corrupted by its deceitful desires; to be made new in the attitude of your minds; and to put on the new self, created to be like God in true righteousness and holiness."

It's Going to Be Okay

Forgiving Your Weakness

If we are solely focused on living in perfection, then we deprive ourselves of the opportunity to experience the holiness of our struggles. Frequently, our own development takes place within the context of our imperfections.

Rabbi Rochelle Robins, *Jewish Pastoral Care*

It was late summer, and I (Steven) was on vacation with my family at a pristine, spring-fed lake in Michigan. I'd left the Thursday night X3LA Recovery Group in the hands of Alex. Alex had been sober from pornography for three years and was the perfect candidate to lead the group.

This lake was in a fairly remote area with limited internet access, so I was able to check my email only a couple of times during the trip. On a warm Wednesday evening, my family and I hiked up to a park where the kids could play and I could download my emails. Tucked within the spam and other e-solicitations was a message from Aaron, a member of the X3LA Recovery Group:

Hello, Steven,

I will not be coming this Thursday. Things are NOT good for me right now. I've been stressed out over a few things and I had a setback the other day. I knew I should have called but I didn't. And I just don't feel like I should be there Thursday, not because I don't want to, but I am too ashamed to show up.

I'm in the middle of trying to find a place to live in the next few months. Something happened in which I was supposed to move in with a friend and he changed his mind at the last minute and my present roommates already found a replacement. So, I have another month to stay at the place and then, I am on my own. Plus there are some other things I need to work out. I've been thinking about calling that counseling number. I just might do so.

At the moment, Steven, I feel very discouraged and without a friend in the world. Just my thoughts at the moment.

That night, I took a moment to step out onto the deck of our rented cabin to call Aaron. Overlooking the calm waters of a peaceful nighttime lake, I waited for Aaron to answer. When he did, the clamor of the Los Angeles freeway, where Aaron was at the time, flooded my ear.

In a calm and friendly voice I told Aaron who was calling, and he settled in for a much-dreaded call. I tried to put Aaron's mind at ease by keeping a sense of humor and painting a word picture of the lake I was currently enjoying with its cool breeze and quiet air.

> *I had a setback the other day. . . . I am too ashamed to show up.*

In between the roar of passing semis, Aaron expressed his sense of shame, failure, and confusion in having returned to pornography. I listened, validating Aaron's feelings, before getting to the matter at hand. I explained in no uncertain terms that Aaron should not feel that he wouldn't be welcome at recovery group, *nor was he to think that there was any other option available to him other than attending.*

About two weeks prior to this phone call, Chris, another member of the X3LA Recovery Group, had to come to a group meeting and admit to having returned to using pornography. Responding to the first statement on our group's Meeting Statement Sheet (see the end of chapter 6), Chris was required to state his first name and how long he had been sober. It was not easy for him to admit to a group of men with whom he had become close friends and who thought he had made so much progress that, only two days prior to that moment, he had used pornography.

What Aaron missed, and what I quickly pointed out, was that night was one of the most important nights for Chris in terms of his recovery. In showing up to the group and being honest, Chris discovered three very important things:

1. His group of like-minded supporters didn't judge or ridicule him and loved him just as he is.
2. He must *consistently* attend recovery group meetings whether he likes it or not. That is one of the places where the pressure and lies of pornography's pull will be released and disabled.
3. Maintaining his sobriety was going to be a continual, lifelong process and *not* an overnight miracle.

It was no mystery that the same week both Chris *and* Aaron had returned to using pornography was the same week they had both failed to attend recovery group.

Forgiving Your Weakness

I wrapped up our phone conversation with words of affirmation, hoping my description of the tranquility of the lake had given Aaron a sense that there is more to life than his weakness that plagued him. I hoped Aaron could see through me a different way of thinking, living, and being.

Sometimes all you need is an opportunity to stop moving, see the world through different eyes, and take a deep breath. Sometimes that's what you need to get the strength and conviction to remain sober. *It is exactly this viewpoint that makes recovery group attendance so incredibly important, whether you feel like going at the moment or not.*

Maintaining sobriety is a continual, lifelong process.

Aaron did attend recovery group the very next night. Alex, my substitute, called Aaron that same day and had a good conversation, and Aaron was prepared to discuss his moment of weakness with the group. Through that experience he found more support, a better perspective, and increased courage to prevail.

Even so, Aaron struggled emotionally during the following week. He knew better than to return to using pornography, but still, the challenges, frustrations, and struggles he was experiencing in his life brought him again to a point where he felt extremely vulnerable and upset. He incorrectly saw his struggle as failure. Fortunately, Aaron had learned the lesson that his recovery group attendance was central to his recovery. No matter how he was feeling, good or bad, he was going to attend.

At the next small group meeting, Aaron shared his feelings of failure, failure in his professional life and failure in terms of his sobriety. Essentially, he was still hanging on to his perception of what his life was supposed to be like instead of God's perception.

Despite all that had been said, Aaron had not yet quite grasped the concept that to be free of pornography, and the causes that lead him to using it, he needed to accept that he is *dead to this world.* If he is truly dead to what he wants from life, dead to his image of what his life is supposed to be like, and dead to the expectations that the world puts on him, he can be made free of all of the pressures that have led him to using pornography.

As we have stated repeatedly in this book, as a Christian, Aaron must accept that he is dead to this world but alive in Christ, alive in all of the wonderful things that Christ has for him, including friends, family, growth, hope, and service. It is no wonder that all four of the Gospels quote Christ, in one form or another, as saying, "Whoever finds his life will lose it, and whoever loses his life for my sake will find it" (Matt. 10:39; see also 16:25; Mark 8:35; Luke 9:24; 17:33; John 12:25).

I felt I was getting through to Aaron but not entirely. And then Trent spoke up.

Trent

Trent is just about the happiest man you could ever meet. He is young, funny, and hopeful. Working as a trainer in a Los Angeles gym, he often jokes that his job specializing in "sculpting women's gluteus maximus muscles" might just be a sexual trigger.

Trent had been sober for ninety days during that meeting, and when he began speaking, not only to Aaron but also to another group member who had recently returned to using pornography, his tone broadcast clearly that he had something important to say, something important *and* personal.

It's like removing a filthy bandage from a dirty, sticky, infected wound.

Calmly, Trent repeated a metaphor another counselor had explained to him that had given him a great deal of perspective. He said that when you remove something like pornography from your life, it's like removing a filthy bandage from a dirty, sticky, infected wound. The only thing that bandage was doing was preventing the wound from healing, allowing it to fester and grow into an unrecognizable sore. To truly let that wound heal, if only into a scar, requires that you remove the bandage so that air, ointment, and appropriate care can reach it.

Trent looked with conviction and determination at Aaron and the other men in the room, his carefree demeanor gone. This was serious.

Then he shared for the first time that he had been sexually abused as a child. In addition to this abuse, his parents, both drug addicts, abandoned him and entered rehab when he was an adolescent. As a way of coping with his confused emotions and hurts, Trent went through years of aggressively acting out sexually, including engaging in anonymous sex, phone sex, and pornography. In addition to this self-abuse, he used food to mask his pains, adding a hundred pounds to his average frame.

Trent became a Christian at an early age, and while he didn't always walk his walk of faith, he always held on to the fact that he believed in a loving God who had a plan for his life. Once Trent reached a point where he could clearly see that his various compulsive behaviors were not only doing him harm but also keeping him from achieving his God-given purpose, he made a commitment to his sobriety. This was not easy for Trent, as abstaining from anonymous sex, pornography, and compulsive overeating forced him to face the hurts of his past and the fact that he needed to learn how to deal with those hurts in constructive ways.

The constructive ways Trent sought out were counseling at Oasis LA, participation in the X3LA Recovery Group, strict adherence to his Sobriety Sheets, and increased participation in church service and time with God. Trent was desperate to express to Aaron and the other men in the X3LA Recovery Group that one fact surrounded all of the action steps he was currently taking to achieve his sobriety: *For him to become sober, he had to accept that he was now dead to this world, dead to what he wants from it, dead to what he expects to* get from it, but deeply, profoundly, and hopefully alive in Christ and all of the promises that come along with belief in him as his Lord and Savior.

"If free will allowed that man to sexually abuse me," he said, "and if free will allowed my parents to choose drugs over me, then I don't want free will. I want God's will."

Coming to this realization hasn't always been an easy process for Trent. One evening after the X3LA Recovery Group, Trent, so upset at having to share and face his pains and hurts, especially in a group setting, went home and ate everything in his refrigerator, then puked it all back up again.

Admittedly, this was not a good coping mechanism for Trent. The goal in recovering from pornography addiction is to replace destructive behavior with constructive behavior. Regardless of this fact, Trent's reaction at having to face the causes of his pornography addiction without indulging himself demonstrates the struggle many men have when facing the causes behind their substance abuse.

I don't want free will.

I want God's will.

Trent is doing much better now. He has learned to keep that filthy bandage of substance abuse off the hurts and struggles that lie deep within his soul. Sure, there are times when facing these things is just too painful for him, and he would like to return to food, pornography, or anonymous sex to soothe his emotions. Instead, he chooses to turn to God, his church, his support group, and his life's purpose. As he does these things, he is finding himself in a place of increased peace, self-knowledge, and hope. His walk is not easy, but it gets easier each day.

But let's let Trent talk about it in his own words:

The idea of recovery was very foreign to me. When I think about recovery, I assume it's for the soccer mom who needs a drink because her husband is never home or the gambler who just can't say no to the bookie. I never thought it would be me, the twenty-seven-year-old college grad at the prime of his life. No kids, no wife, and all the freedom available at my fingertips. And that was my problem: exercising too much freedom. At twenty-seven years old, I was watching porn all the time, having casual (sometimes anonymous) sex, and building unhealthy relationships with my friends and family. I needed help.

I realized that my troubled childhood filled with sexual and emotional abuse was a root problem. I realized that misguided decisions and carelessness led me down this troubled path, but somehow God's mercy and grace never left me.

This book [*Pure Eyes*], my recovery group, and my counselor have helped me look at the world differently. I'm learning to build healthy relationships and I have realized that as a child of God I must have respect for myself and respect the people around me. I've learned that accountability is important and that I am not alone in my struggle. Every day I am faced with new challenges and the struggle is not over, but I am prepared to face the challenge with God's Word, amazing people by my side, and this book, a reminder that recovery is possible and that a bright future lies ahead.

My values are different. I look forward to marriage and having kids one day and I know that getting away from porn and building healthy relationships will equip me for that journey. The biggest change for me is my outlook on life and my relationship with God. I respect myself, and my love for God manifests itself in admiration for him, obedience to his Word, and constant fellowship with his children. I thirst for his teachings and want to be like King David, a man after God's own heart.

All in all I am excited about the future. I know God will prevail and that I will beat this addiction. I know that his will is going to be done and that I will be blessed and able to do his work here on earth.

Sobriety Checklist

We shared Aaron's and Trent's testimonies to show that both men have now arrived at the place where *all* men who are recovering from addictions to pornography need to arrive. They have now realized that there is never, ever a reason to use pornography. For them now there is never, ever an excuse to continue to bury what has happened to them and to turn their back on God by choosing substances of abuse.

Is it going to be challenging? Yes. Is it going to require attending weekly recovery group meetings whether they want to or not? Of course. Will it require that they gain outside counseling through their church or other counseling centers? Maybe. But the rewards are there.

Are you honestly doing the things we have proposed in this book? We offer you a simple checklist to help you in times of anguish, struggle, confusion, or setback. It is a summary of the basic steps required to achieve freedom from porn. If you aren't experiencing freedom, you now know what piece may be missing from your recovery program. Don't hesitate to start including it in your daily life.

And remember: when you experience anguish, torment, triggers, or the occasional setback, *that's your chance to pinpoint the real cause of your addiction.* This isn't a football game where one side wins and the other loses; recovery is more like a good novel where the hero (you) gradually works through challenges to grow and change and eventually achieve peace.

◆■◆

Sobriety Checklist

- ✗ I have and maintain an accountability partner whom I may call at any time, day or night.
- ✗ I have prepared my Sobriety Sheets, paying close attention to list all of my sexual triggers and environmental and emotional nonsexual triggers.

✗ I have made a list of the remedy actions I can take to avoid my triggers.

✗ When I am triggered, I turn to my Escape Plan and follow it, including:
  • diverting my thoughts
  • praying to God
  • calling my accountability partner
  • finding a God-sanctioned activity, including my life's purpose, to refocus my mind

✗ After having been triggered, I have reviewed my Sobriety Sheets to make sure they include the trigger that caused my sexual arousal and a corresponding remedy action. If not, I have added it.

✗ I am actively involved in a pornography recovery small group, one that uses as its guide the Meeting Statement Sheet.

✗ I am currently enlarging my faith by:
  • reading Scripture daily
  • praying daily
  • attending church weekly
  • attending a weekly small group or Bible study
  • serving God
  • tithing
  • fasting monthly or weekly
  • respecting the Sabbath

◆■◆

If you are doing these things but not finding healing, please seek out professional one-on-one counseling. Most certainly your church will have resources available to you. Additionally, XXXchurch.com provides access to innumerable resources that may be available in your region.

Chris

We conclude with a testimony from Chris, the man who came to me a few years back and helped spark the series of events that led to the writing of this book. When Chris came to my office years ago to ask for help with his pornography addiction, he got far more than he bargained for. At the time he had no idea I was involved with XXXchurch, nor did he know that I would be so open to helping him with his challenge.

Chris's journey over the past few years has been an interesting one, with advances and setbacks, twists and turns. But through it all, he has hung on to the central principle that will eventually get him to his sobriety: *commitment*. Despite mistakes and successes, Chris held on to the belief that, if he ever wants to be free from pornography, he has to keep getting back on his horse each and every time he gets bucked off.

Since this project began because of Chris, we feel it is only fitting to end it with his testimony, a testimony that we trust will give encouragement and hope to those of you starting on your journey to sobriety:

For so many years, I had struggled alone with a pornography addiction. I didn't believe that confessing my problem to anyone was an option. I had been a Christian from a young age and lived a life with strong convictions about purity. Even through my struggles, I never doubted the fact that my actions were sinful. Because of that, I was left feeling isolated, wanting to battle this force that would have pulled me back into sin but knowing I was on my own. The addiction continued for fifteen years. Sometimes it would become seemingly dormant (though usually for not more than a few months), and most other times it would rage in me, inducing weeklong binges of pornography and masturbation. As a result, my emotional life was a wreck. My self-esteem (the little that was there) was constantly under fire by the knowledge that, while I believed my desires and actions to consume pornography were wrong, I lacked the ability to effectively control them. I felt powerless.

A hypocrite. I would surely have encouraged anyone else to abandon all such behavior at any cost, but when it came to my own life, that didn't seem to be a viable option.

About fifteen years into my addiction cycle, I hit a breaking point. My wife, who had known about the problem and tried to be a support for me, was quickly losing her patience and hoped that this problem would dissipate. I needed to find an accountability partner who wasn't as emotionally invested in me as my wife, because her waning ability to maintain a position of objectivity about my addiction was beginning to complicate things. It was becoming apparent that my wife, who (being a victim of sexual abuse as a child) had her own challenges to deal with in the area of sexuality, was (with no fault of her own) unable to help me with my problem without impeding the progress of her own sexual healing journey.

After mustering up the strength to take the plunge and entrust my accountability to my friend Steven, I found myself in a new place where I was able to share every salacious detail of my thoughts, desires, and actions with someone whom I knew would not respond emotionally. Here was a person who loved me and did not condemn me, and was willing to help me fight this addiction and start "getting to the bottom of things." He saw things I couldn't see. He offered advice that would never have occurred to me. He was able to have a clear mind about the issue, one that wasn't fogged up and stifled from an ongoing addiction cycle. For the first time in fifteen years, I really felt that something new was happening. I might actually have a chance to beat this thing.

Here was a person who loved me and did not condemn me.

After a few months of meeting with Steven, he suggested that our one-on-one meetings be expanded to a group setting so more men could benefit from this accountability. A biweekly group was formed and within a month, we had half a dozen men attending. This format offered yet another helpful perspective that was lacking from my personal meetings with Steven. For the first time, I was sitting in a safe environment with like-minded men who shared a common struggle, and listening to *their* stories. As they bravely shared their stories, I began to realize how much their struggle against this addiction resembled my own.

As the weeks went on, we began to adopt the word 'sobriety' as something we all were aiming to maintain with regard to our pornography addiction. Through Steven's research and interviews with a psychiatrist and a sex therapist, we began to gain an understanding of the physiological effects that pornography consumption and masturbation have on the brain.

We also were introduced to a plan for maintaining a freedom from pornography addiction. Through this plan, we were reminded that, although there was a physiological element to this addiction, more importantly there was a spiritual aspect that could not be ignored. For the first time in my life, I was able to understand why I experienced the immense desire to run back to pornography (the physiological dependence), and was also able to counteract the desires with mental and physical reminders of my purpose in life. I was encouraged to discover the various triggers in my life that would start me down that same insidious path again and develop action plans for each of them.

As our group made progress, we realized the need to start meeting weekly instead of biweekly. We continue helping each other stay focused on the *truth* and keep our heads clear from the "fog of war" that can descend from the constant battle of this addiction.

I am encouraged because I don't feel isolated anymore. Through the care and compassion of the men in my group, I am not only being equipped to more effectively battle my own addiction, but also to be available to help other men who might be struggling quietly as I was. If you are struggling alone with this addiction, I encourage you to take that first bold step out of the shadows and begin to see the freedom that is within reach.

I don't feel isolated anymore.

Find a support group like the one described in this book that will receive you with compassion and understanding and will help you regain and maintain your footing while encouraging you to fix your sights on God's purpose for your life.

God bless you.

Appendix

Sobriety Sheets

- - - - - - - - - -

Creating a Victorious Environment

Sexual Triggers

1. _____
2. _____
3. _____
4. _____
5. _____

Remedy Actions

1. _____
2. _____
3. _____
4. _____
5. _____

Nonsexual Environmental Triggers

1. _____
2. _____
3. _____
4. _____
5. _____

Remedy Actions

1. _____
2. _____
3. _____
4. _____
5. _____

Nonsexual Emotional Triggers

1. _____
2. _____
3. _____
4. _____
5. _____

Remedy Actions

1. _____
2. _____
3. _____
4. _____
5. _____

- - - - - - - - - -

Escape Plan

I. Mental and Physical Reminders

   1. _____

    _____

   2. _____

    _____

   3. _____

    _____

   4. _____

    _____

   5. _____

    _____

II. Confession

   1. To God

   2. To your accountability partner: _____

III. Focus on the "Yes" (any God-honoring activity)

   1. Your purpose: _____

    _____

   2. _____

    _____

   3. _____

    _____

   4. _____

    _____

   5. _____

    _____

IV. Revisit and Update Trigger Lists

Notes

1. Judith A. Reisman, PhD, *The Psychopharmacology of Pictorial Pornography Restructuring Brain, Mind & Memory & Subverting Freedom of Speech* (New York: The Institute for Media Education, 2003).

2. Michael J. Bader, *Arousal: The Secret Logic of Sexual Fantasies* (New York: St. Martin's Press, 2002), 17–24.

3. Go to http://www.ojp.usdoj.gov/bjs/crimoff.htm.

Resources

Online

www.XXXchurch.com

www.x3pure.com (30 days to purity workshop)

www.everymansbattle.com

www.purelifeministries.org

www.higher-calling.com

www.sash.net (Society for the Advancement of Sexual Health)

www.slaafws.org (Sex and Love Addicts Anonymous)

www.sexhelp.com (Dr. Patrick Carnes Sexual Addiction Resources)

Books

Recovery

Arterburn, Stephen. *Every Man's Battle: Winning the War on Sexual Temptation One Victory at a Time.* Colorado Springs: WaterBrook Press, 2000.

Black, Claudia, PhD. *It Will Never Happen to Me: Growing Up with Addiction as Youngsters, Adolescents, Adults.* Center City, MN: Hazelden, 2001.

Carnes, Patrick, PhD. *Facing the Shadow: Starting Sexual and Relationship Recovery,* 2nd ed. Carefree, AZ: Gentle Path Press, 2008.

Carnes, Patrick, Debra Laaser, and Mark Laaser. *Open Hearts: Renewing Relationships with Recovery, Romance and Reality.* Carefree, AZ: Gentle Path Press, 1999.

Earle, Ralph H., and Mark R. Laaser. *The Pornography Trap: Setting Pastors and Laypersons Free from Sexual Addiction.* Kansas City: Beacon Hill Press, 2002.

Gallagher, Steve. *Out of the Depths of Sexual Sin.* Dry Ridge, KY: Pure Life Ministries, 2003.

Maltz, Wendy, and Larry Maltz. *The Porn Trap: The Essential Guide to Overcoming Problems Caused by Pornography.* New York: Harper Collins, 2008.

Schnarch, David. *Intimacy and Desire.* New York: Beaufort Books, 2009.

Faith

Answers in the Heart: Daily Meditations for Men and Women Recovering from Sex Addiction. Center City, MN: Hazelden, 1989.

Gross, Craig. *Dirty Little Secret.* Grand Rapids: Zondervan, 2006.

Hope and Recovery: The Twelve-Step Guide for Healing from Compulsive Sexual Behavior. Center City, MN: Hazelden, 1994.

Nouwen, Henri. *Reaching Out: The Three Movements of the Spiritual Life.* Garden City, NY: Doubleday, 1986.

_____. *The Return of the Prodigal Son: A Story of Homecoming.* New York: Doubleday, 1986.

Palmer, Parker J. *A Hidden Wholeness: The Journey toward an Undivided Life*. San Francisco: John Wiley and Sons, 2004.

_____. *Let Your Life Speak: Listening for the Voice of Vocation*. San Francisco: John Wiley and Sons, 1999.

Software

Accountability Software: X3watch, www.x3watch.com

Internet Filtering Software: Safe Eyes, www.safeeyes.com/xxxchurch

Recovery Groups

Celebrate Recovery, www.celebraterecovery.com

LIFE Ministries, www.freedomeveryday.org

Sexaholics Anonymous, www.sa.org

Sex Addicts Anonymous, www.saa-recovery.org

Live-in Programs

Pure Life Ministries, www.purelifeministries.org

Bethesda Workshops, www.bethesdaworkshops.org

Serenity Prayer

God, grant me the Serenity
To accept the things I cannot change . . .
Courage to change the things I can,
And Wisdom to know the difference.

Living one day at a time,
Enjoying one moment at a time,
Accepting hardship as the pathway to peace.
Taking, as He did, this sinful world as it is,
Not as I would have it.
Trusting that He will make all things right
if I surrender to His will.
That I may be reasonably happy in this life,
And supremely happy with Him forever in the next.
Amen.

—Reinhold Niebuhr

Acknowledgments

This book would not have been possible without the help and support of Pastor Philip Wagner of Oasis Church in Los Angeles; Steven Kiefer, who has helped lead the X3LA Recovery Groups for over two years; all of the men who came through the X3LA Recovery Groups and shared their stories; editor Adam Palmer; and our wives, Jeanette and Rundi, who supported us as we supported others.

Craig Gross founded Fireproof Ministries and XXXchurch. com and is the author of several books, including *The Dirty Little Secret: Uncovering the Truth Behind Porn*; *Questions You Can't Ask Your Mama about Sex*; and *Starving Jesus.* He currently lives in Los Angeles with his wife, Jeanette, and two kids, Nolan and Elise.

www.XXXchurch.com
www.craiggross.com

Steven Luff, MDiv, MA, is a registered marriage and family therapist intern. Since 2008, he has led sexual addiction recovery groups affiliated with xxxchurch.com. Steven is the creator of the X3Pure 30 Days to Purity online recovery program. Currently he sees clients and he blogs for the Faith and Sex Center in Los Angeles, California. Steven lives in Santa Monica with his wife and two children.

FROM CRAIG GROSS, FOUNDER OF XXXCHURCH.COM

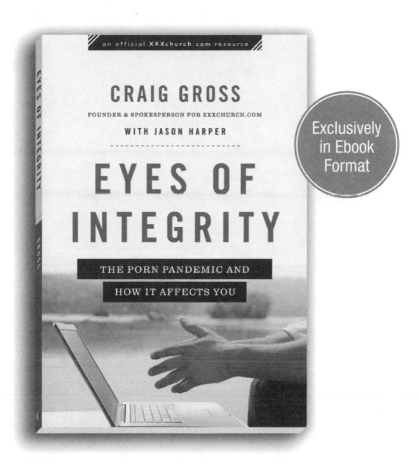

Learn about the reach and consequences of sexual addiction in our society, our churches, and our families, and what you can do to help stop it.

An Open, Honest, and Biblically Based Guide for Women

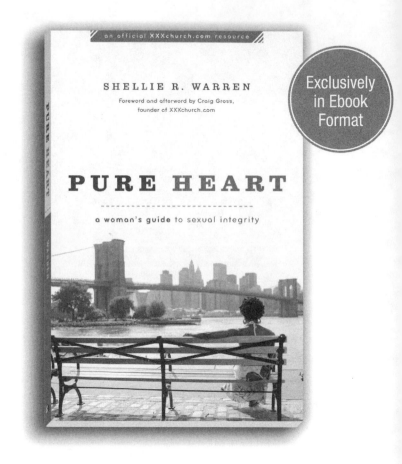

an official XXXchurch.com resource

SHELLIE R. WARREN

Foreword and afterword by Craig Gross, founder of XXXchurch.com

PURE HEART

a woman's guide to sexual integrity

Exclusively in Ebook Format

In this frank and disarming book, Shellie Warren speaks to women from her own life experiences and helps women understand and embrace the true purpose of sex in their lives.

BakerBooks
a division of Baker Publishing Group
www.BakerBooks.com

Go to XXXchurch.com for the tools you need to respond to the porn pandemic. These resources, specifically designed for individuals, couples, families, and churches, are not available anywhere else.

This website is updated daily with helps and resources for parents, women, men, youth, spouses, pastors, and more. Join the discussion! **www.xxxchurch.com**

Free accountability software available from XXXchurch or with purchase of *Eyes of Integrity*. This software automatically emails a selected accountability partner whenever a questionable internet site has been accessed. This information is meant to encourage open and honest conversation between friends and help us all be more accountable. **www.x3watch.com**

Offers 30-day online workshops featuring Steven Luff and Shellie R. Warren. These frank and open discussions are excellent companions to *Pure Eyes* and *Pure Heart*. **www.x3pure.com**

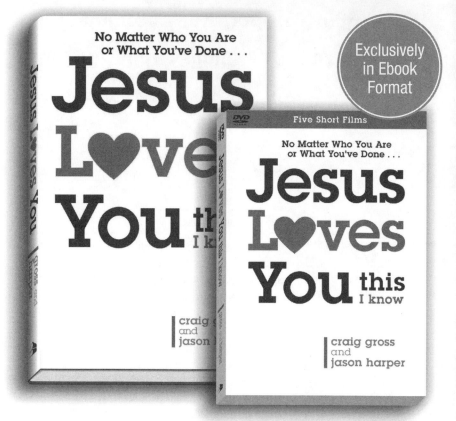